Chambers

BOOK OF SPORTS FACTS

Nimish Dubey and Akriti Rana are one of the best-known joint bylines and writing teams in the Indian media space. Based in Delhi, both have studied communications and have been working together on journalistic as well as corporate projects for almost a decade now.

They have been widely published in the *Indian Express*, *ABPLive*, *Huffington Post*, *India Today* and *91Mobiles*. They like words and wordplay, love music and are very fond of animals. No cat or dog can pass within a hundred yards of them without being petted endlessly.

Chambers BOOK OF SPORTS FACTS

NIMISH DUBEY
AKRITI RANA

hachette INDIA

First published in 2024 by Hachette India
(Registered name: Hachette Book Publishing India Pvt. Ltd)
An Hachette UK company
www.hachetteindia.com

Chambers® is a registered trademark of Chambers Harrap Publishers Ltd,
an Hachette UK company

1

Text provided by Nimish Dubey and Akriti Rana

ISBN 978-93-5731-363-6

Hachette Book Publishing India Pvt. Ltd
4th & 5th Floors, Corporate Centre
Plot No. 94, Sector 44, Gurugram – 122003, India

Typeset in Adobe Garamond Pro 11/13.2
by Manmohan Kumar, Delhi

Printed and bound in India
by Manipal Technologies Limited

FSC www.fsc.org
MIX
Paper | Supporting responsible forestry
FSC™ C043100

Contents

Preface

The word 'sports' has a slightly flippant, throwaway air about it. It is often clubbed with 'pastime', making it seem like some sort of a hobby or a distraction. Dictionaries define the term sport as 'a physical or athletic activity engaged in for pleasure'. Even the topic itself is considered a secondary one for discussion by some, after all the 'serious' stuff like politics and business.

On the contrary, there is so much more to sports than just two teams or individuals trying to outshine the other in some regard. It may sound cliché, but sports actually is a reflection of life, complete with struggle, friendship, villainy, success and failure, and all the other hues that are part of true human existence. And these are experienced not only by those who play, but those who watch them as well.

Chambers Book of Sports Facts brings all these varied and wonderful aspects of sport to the readers. The book is not about records, although they do appear in their fair share, or just the best and brightest from the world of sports. It is a collection of vignettes, incidents, quotes and much more from the whole width of the sporting spectrum, irrespective of region or time, collated and curated from a host of sources, both modern and ancient.

You will read about not just modern legends like Usain Bolt (who literally lived on McDonald's chicken nuggets for days before a major race), but also about Kynisca, the sister of the King of Sparta, who was the first woman Olympic champion (way back in 396 BCE). It is not just about champions, but also about those who took part and tried their best, and in some cases, those who perhaps did not even realize that they were making a difference to the world of sports – ask Pickles, the dog who literally saved the 1966 World Cup by discovering the trophy that had been stolen on the eve of the tournament.

There is wit and whimsy as well – Pierre Coquelin de Lisle sending a wire to his mum 'Am an Olympic champion. World record beaten. Will arrive Tuesday morning' in 1924; India's Mansoor Ali Khan Pataudi aka Tiger Pataudi, saying he realized he could play with one eye when he saw the state of the English bowling attack, and others.

It is not all roses, though.

Sports has its share of controversies and tragedies, and you will find plenty of them in the pages that follow, from the infamous drug controversies of Ben Johnson at the 1984 Olympic Games to Lance Armstrong more than a decade later.

But most important of all, there is heroism and nobility. You will read of the Olympic champion who stopped rowing to let ducks pass, the lone runner who kept going even after the winners had crossed the line because 'my country didn't send me 7,000 miles to start the race. They sent me 7,000 miles to finish it', the woman who was paralysed below her knees but still beat men at the Olympics and more.

Perspiration, inspiration, genius, skullduggery, loyalty, victory, defeat...they are all as much a part of sports as they are of life. You will find plenty of each in the pages that unfold. The word 'sports' might have a flippant, throwaway air about it to some, but to those who know it, it is life. Liverpool Football Club's legendary manager Bill Shankly was once asked if football was a matter of life and death for him. He is believed to have replied:

'Nay, lad. It's much more important than that.'

It indeed can be!

CHAPTER ONE

Basics and Beginnings

The Man Who Made the Olympic Games Possible

The Olympic Games are easily the most prestigious multi-sport sporting event in the world. And we owe their existence to the persistence of a French educator and historian. Pierre de Coubertin (1863–1937) was born Pierre de Fredy in an aristocratic family in France. He got the idea of the Olympic Games while studying law and public affairs at the Paris Institute of Political Studies. A firm believer in sport having a positive effect on human life, Coubertin idolized ancient Greece, many believe even to an unrealistic extent. He got the idea of reviving the Olympic Games, which were at that time a part of ancient Greek history, in 1889 and spent years getting support from athletes and administrative bodies. After a number of disputes and disappointments, an agreement was finally reached in 1894 at Sorbonne that the modern Olympic Games would take place in Athens in 1896 and in Paris in 1900. The International Olympic Committee (IOC) was formed to administer the Games, with Greek businessman Dimitrios Vikélas named as its first president as Greece would host the first Games. Coubertin would be the second President of the IOC. The modern Olympic Games faced a number of challenges (1900, 1904 and 1908 were organizational disasters), but after the initial stutters, became an integral part of the global sports calendar, and indeed, its crown jewel. Today, winning an Olympic medal is supposed to be the greatest achievement in the life of an athlete, and it all happened because a French man in the nineteenth century believed that sport ennobled people.

No Fighting during the Olympics

In ancient times, the Olympic Games were considered sacred because they were held in honour of the king of gods, Zeus. Therefore, a period of truce was declared for the duration of the Games, and athletes and their families were guaranteed safe passage. No one was allowed to carry weapons inside the venue of the Games, and even executions were postponed.

The Olympics for Women… Sort of

While women were not allowed as participants or even as spectators at the ancient Olympics, they did have a sporting event of their own. These were the Heraean Games that were also held at four-year intervals, like the Olympics, and were hosted at Olympia. There was only one sport at these Games, which were held in honour of the goddess Hera – a foot race, or a stadion, as it was called. Only unmarried young women were allowed to compete, and races were held in three different age categories. The winners received a crown of olive leaves, a portion of a cow sacrificed to the goddess and also a statue dedicating themselves to Hera.

Number of Events in the Olympics? Well, in the Beginning There Was Just One!

Today, the Olympics usually have 40 different sports and more than 400 events. But it was not always thus. In fact, in their initial period (starting from 776 BC), the Olympics had only one event. This was a foot race called the stade, which was a 192-metre sprint on rolled sand. It was run barefoot. Other events are believed to have been added in 724 BC.

How Many Sports Are There in the Olympics NOW?

There are hundreds of sports all around the world, but not all of them make it to the Olympic Games. The 2020 edition (held in 2021), the Olympic Games had a total of 40 sports – 32 in the summer Olympics, and eight in the Winter Olympics.

The Two Nations That Have Been at Every Olympics

The Olympic Games might be the world's premier sporting event, but they have seen their share of controversies and disputes. Many of these have led to countries boycotting the Games or refusing to send their athletes to a particular Games. However, two nations have always participated in the Olympics. They have been in every Olympic Games from 1896 onwards – Greece and Australia.

Why Is Sword Fighting Called Fencing? Blame Shakespeare

Why is the art of sword fighting called 'fencing' and not, well, 'sword fighting' or 'sword combat' or something that seems a bit more direct. Well, evidently, it is because it is derived from the Latin term 'defensa', which means 'protection', which in turn led to the French term 'defens' with a similar meaning. The British further shortened it to 'fens', and when a character in Shakespeare's play *The Merry Wives of Windsor* said in reference to swordsmanship, 'Alas, sir, I cannot fence', the term was official.

Running, Horse Riding, Sword Fighting – the Insanity of the Modern Pentathlon

In terms of sheer variety, no sporting event can perhaps match the modern pentathlon, which consists of a number of sports that the participants have to take part in over a very short period of time. Broadly, this is what every participant in the modern pentathlon has to do:

- Two rounds of epee fencing, one of a minute (or until the first hit) and one of 45 seconds, where a contestant has to combat every other contestant. So, if there are ten contestants, each will have nine fencing contests at least.
- A 200 metres freestyle swim.
- Riding a horse over a show jumping course with 12 obstacles. Contestants cannot bring their own horses to the event and are allotted horses at random. They have 20 minutes to practise with their horse before the event.
- A combined running and shooting event, where each contestant runs 3,200 metres, stopping four times to shoot at targets with laser pistols for up to 50 seconds!

Whatever a modern pentathlete can complain of, it is certainly not a lack of variety of sport.

The Origin of Table Tennis – It Lies in Books

Imagine a sport that was played with books. Literally. Well, it is believed that the origin of table tennis owes a lot to books. By many accounts, the game was popular among British officers in India in the 1860s and 1870s, who played it on a table, using a row of books placed spine upwards as a net and books as rackets to hit a golf ball back and forth!

'Thou Shalt Not Advise Thy Opponent' – Yes, Golf Has a Rule for That!

Baron Pierre de Coubertin might have believed that sport enables friendships and comradeship, but there are some sports that

Statue of Baron Pierre de Coubertin in Olympic Centennial Park

actually levy a penalty if you help your opponent with some well-meant advice. The most famous is golf, which clearly states that a player cannot seek advice from anyone other than their own caddie, playing partner or playing partner's caddie. The person giving advice or assistance is penalized a stroke, although the receiver is not penalized initially!

Keep Your Hat on in Tennis or Lose the Point!

If you are wearing a cap or hat while playing tennis, remember to keep it firmly on. If it falls off in the course of a match, your opponent can ask for the point to be replayed.

No Men Allowed – Olympic Sports Only Women Can Participate in

In the beginning, women were prevented from taking part in most sports of the Olympic Games. Today, they take part in most sports and even have some sports that only they can participate in. In the 2020 Tokyo Olympics (which were ultimately held in 2021 because of the COVID epidemic), there were three sports exclusively for women – artistic swimming (also called synchronized swimming), softball and rhythmic gymnastics.

Popular? Yes, but Not in the Olympics: Ten Popular Sports That Are Not Proper Olympic Sports

The Olympic Games do not include a number of very popular sports. The reasons for this vary from politics to administrative issues. Some sports get included for a short duration but are then excluded. As per the information on last and the 2024 edition, the following sports were not included in the Olympic Games despite having a considerable following:

1. Cricket
2. Squash
3. Netball
4. Bowling
5. Mixed Martial Arts
6. Billiards
7. American Football
8. Chess
9. Darts
10. Rugby Union

A Medical Condition Named after a Sport

It is technically called lateral epicondylitis and refers to a condition in which a person has to endure a lot of pain on the outside of the elbow. It occurs because of overuse of the muscles of the forearm, near the elbow. But its more common name is tennis elbow. The reason is simple – it used to occur very frequently in tennis players!

When Jerseys Got Numbers

These days it is common to see almost every athlete in sport (especially team sports) playing with a number on their back. Some sports even have the names of the players on their jerseys. These numbers are generally placed to identify a player and their position in a team. Teams started using numbers on their jerseys in the early part of the twentieth century, and the first recorded instance of this is supposed to be in a rugby match between Queensland and New Zealand in 1897.

TEN Sports Rolled into One

The most strenuous event in athletics is the decathlon. As its name indicates, it comprises a total of ten sports, and athletes are awarded points for their performance in each sport. The ten sports are held over two days and comprise the 100-metre sprint, 400-metre sprint, long jump, shot-put, high jump, 110-metre hurdles, discus throw, pole vault, javelin throw and finally, the run. In the Olympic Games, the decathlon is an event only for men, with women participating in a seven-event version called the heptathlon, but there are indications that the decathlon will be opened to women as well in the coming editions of the Games.

The Net That Dips in the Middle

One of the most common tips you will get from tennis coaches is to hit the ball over the middle of the net. The reason for this is simple – tennis, for some very odd reason, has a net that is taller at the sides and is lowest in the middle. A tennis net is three feet six inches tall near the posts and is three feet in the middle. A band attached to the court actually pulls down the middle of the net to a lower height! So tennis coaches advise players to hit the ball 'down the middle' because that is the lowest part of the net, and so, the ball stands the best chance of clearing it.

Want a Fair Trial? Let's Discus… Out of Court

Rather intriguingly, each effort in the discus throw event is not called an effort or even an attempt. It is called a trial! Talk of athletic justice.

Dojo Kun – the Code of Karate

It might be a martial art and revolve around striking your opponent, but Karate has a deep, spiritual side and is actually seen as a means of self-development. The word 'karate' literally means 'open hand', and the sport has its own Dojo Kun, or a code or set of guidelines that has to be followed by all its practitioners in their lives. It is often recited before and after training sessions and has nothing whatsoever to do with fighting:

- Seek perfection of character
- Be faithful
- Endeavour
- Respect others
- Refrain from violent behaviour

The Three Swords of Fencing, and What They Are Allowed to Touch

Competitive fencing is done with three kinds of swords. And interestingly, all three have different target areas in terms of scoring. Yes, the aim with all three is to register a 'touch' on the opponent, but there is a little more to it than that. So here is a simple summary of the kind of swords used in fencing and how they score points:

- Foil: About 500 gm in weight, it is considered a thrusting weapon and registers touches only with the tip. Touching an opponent with the side does not count. What's more, touches can only be made on the upper body of the opponent, excluding the arms.
- Sabre: Also about 500 gm, the sabre is called a cutting and thrusting weapon. It registers touches not just with the tip but

with the blade as well. A touch can be registered on any part of the upper body of the opponent.

- Épée: At 775 gm, this is the heaviest sword in fencing. Like the foil, is it a thrusting weapon and registers touches only with the tip. But it is the only sword in fencing that is allowed to target the entire body of the opponent – a touch is registered when any part of the body comes in contact with the tip of an épée.

The Combat Sport with No Weight Class

Whether it is boxing, judo, wrestling or taekwondo, most sports that have an element of person-to-person combat in them have different weight categories for competition. One combat sport, however, which has no weight categories and where two people of totally different sizes can 'fight' against each other is fencing. The categories here are determined by the kind of sword used rather than the weight of the competitor.

Football's Indoor Cousin

It might be the most popular sport in the world (as per some), but football has also spawned a very popular cousin, which is mainly played indoors. Called futsal, the sport is played on a smaller area with a smaller ball, between two teams of five players each (including the goalkeeper) over two halves of twenty minutes each. There are unlimited substitutions allowed, and there are many who feel the game actually has greater stress on skill than OG football.

The Man Who Invented Judo

Most sports evolve over a period of time with different social and geographical influences, which makes it difficult to credit a single person with their creation. However, in the case of judo, there is no confusion whatsoever about the sports creator. Everyone agrees that it is Kanō Jigorō (1860–1938), a Japanese educator and athlete.

Want a Hat? Get Three in a Row!

Doing something three times consecutively is referred to as a hat-trick. The term owes its origins to cricket and is believed to have been first used in 1858 when cricketer H.H. Stephenson took three wickets from three consecutive deliveries. The spectators collected money for Stephenson to celebrate the feat and with the proceeds, they bought a hat, which they presented to him. This soon became an accepted practice in cricket, and the term itself moved on to other sports and even life in general for three similar things done in a row, even if one did not get a hat for them!

Why Does Tennis Have That 15, 30, 40 and Love Score System? Tick Tock...

Tennis has a very unique scoring system, which follows a rather odd sequence of numbers. Players start at 'love', get '15' when they win their first point, '30' when they win their second, '40' on winning a third point and generally win a game when they have won a fourth point. Why this system of love, 15, 30, 40, instead of the good old 0, 1, 2, 3… which incidentally is followed not only in most other sports but also in tennis itself when it comes to counting games and sets? Well, it seems to come from the fact that scores were kept on clock faces during the early days of the sport in the fifteenth and sixteenth centuries. With every point, the hand of the clock was moved a quarter hour – so the scoring was 15, 30, 45 and game. They say that when clocks stopped being used and scores started being called out

'45' was altered to '40' to make it easier to speak. And why is zero called 'love'? No, there is nothing deeply philosophical here about the noble sentiment. Many feel that 'love' is actually derived from the French word 'l'oeuf' which means 'egg', which is what a zero looks like. So at the core of the scoring system of one of the most popular sports in the world is a clock and a poultry product!

Why Does the Motor Racing Championship Sound like… Baby Food?

Which sport sounds like something you would feed a baby? Well, it is ironically one of the most hyped and glamorized sports in the world – Formula One racing. It is kind of weird that a sport that has names like Ferrari, Williams, Ford, McLaren, and so many others, has actually that rather tame name tag that sounds like something from a children's ward or a chemistry lab. And no, the sport did not get that name because of some magical research that yielded a special formula. It was far simpler and bureaucratic. While motor racing had been around since the early twentieth century (Sir Arthur Conan Doyle, of Sherlock Holmes fame, was one of its earliest proponents), it started gaining traction in the 1920s and 1930s as cars improved. In the 1930s, the main racing championship was the European Championship and it was organized by the rather complexly named Association Internationale des Automobile Clubs Reconnus (AIACR), which was the sport's governing body.

The outbreak of the Second World War stopped motor racing for a while, and when it was resumed in 1946, steps were taken to change the sport. To start off, the AIACR was rechristened as the Fédération Internationale de l'Automobile (FIA), a name that exists to this day (smaller abbreviations rock!). It was also the time when the idea of having an official world championship came to the fore – a concept often credited to Marquis Antonio Brivio-Sforza, Italy's representative in the FIA. Initially, the championship was supposed to be called Formula Internationale, although Formula A was also considered. The term 'Formula' was favoured because many felt it best represented a racing division (we wonder if they had any infants in the house). By the time the formula (pun intended) for the championship was finalized, 'Formula One' had emerged as the favoured name for it. In 1949, it was finally announced the FIA Formula One World Championship would take place in 1950, with a world champion at the end of the season.

The Sport with No Back Passing

It is a sport that is played with a ball, which has to be put by a team into a goal on the opposite side of the ground. But what makes rugby union very different from many games is the fact that you are not allowed to pass the ball ahead. That's right, in rugby union you cannot pass the ball in the direction of the goal you are attacking. Instead, you are only allowed to pass the ball towards your own goal. You can kick the ball forward, though. Imagine having a rule like that in football or hockey!

The 24-Second Rule That Makes Basketball Such a Fast Sport

Ever wondered why basketball is played at such a frenetic, almost non-stop pace? Well, it is because of something called the 24-second rule. It was introduced in 1954 in the NBA (basketball's most famous league), and according to it, a team that gets possession of the ball has to shoot at the basketball within 24 seconds or else the possession will be turned over to the opposition. A clock actually starts ticking every time the ball changes possession, which is also why sometimes you suddenly see players taking seemingly wild shots – they know their time is limited and is running out. You cannot play to keep possession in NBA basketball.

Why Do Golf Courses Have 18 Holes?

Golf courses as a rule have 18 holes. The question arises: why 18? Well, some say it is because the game originated in Scotland and there are eighteen shots in a bottle of Scotch whisky, so basically, the player could have a quick drink before playing each hole (we do not want to speculate on their condition by the time they reached the end of the course). That story, while high-spirited, is not true. The reality is a trifle more dull. The simple fact is that golf's most respected course, St. Andrews in Scotland (which many call the home of golf) had 18 holes and everyone else simply copied it. Actually, St. Andrews had 22 holes, which were later reduced to 18 in 1764, with four short holes being combined into two. That has been the template most courses have followed ever since. Incidentally, the pub or the bar is referred to as the 19th hole in some courses!

The Distance of the Marathon and the Impact of Royalty

The official distance of the marathon is 42 kilometres and 195 metres, or 26 miles and 385 metres. But why this very odd distance? The race is, of course, inspired by the Greek soldier Pheidippides, who ran the distance from the battlefield of Marathon to Athens (which is around 40 kilometres) to inform the citizens that the Persians had been defeated in a crucial battle in 460 BCE. But the distance of the marathon in the Olympics varied from one Olympics to another – it was 40 kilometres in Athens in 1896, 40.26 kilometres in Paris in 1900, 40 kilometres again in St. Louis in 1904, and 41.86 kilometres in the Intercalated Olympics of 1906. The current distance of 42 kilometres and 195 metres was first used in the 1908 Olympic Games in London, and the reason for the distance had nothing to do with history or athletics. The organizers wanted to start the race from Windsor Castle, the residence of the English royal family and end it at the Royal Box in the White City Stadium – a distance of (you guessed it) 42 kilometres and 195 metres. And although the distance of the marathon went back to 40.2 kilometres in the next Olympics at Stockholm, when the International Amateur Athletic Federation decided to standardize the length of the marathon in 1921, it chose the distance run in the 1908 Olympics at London. No reason was given for choosing this distance, although some feel that the drama that accompanied that race (with one of the competitors, Dorando Pietri, fainting several times before being helped over the line by officials) might have played a role. Still, the length of the marathon might have been different if the Royal Box at the stadium or Windsor Castle had been located at slightly longer or shorter distances!

The Sport You Cannot Play Left-Handed

Being a left-hander is supposed to be an advantage in most sports. So imagine there being a sport where you are not allowed to play left-handed? And it is a well-known sport too – polo. In many countries, you are not allowed to use your left hand to swing the polo stick to strike the ball, simply because a left and a right-hander facing each other on horseback might end up striking each other or each other's horses. It is a safety issue. Some clubs and nations do allow left-handers, though. We do not how quite how the socialists feel about it, but this is literally very much a right-wing game!

A Very Complicated Race

Races do not come more complicated than the 3,000 metres steeplechase. Runners have to run 3,000 metres of course, but what a 3,000 metres it is. They have to negotiate four hurdles on every lap and a 12-foot pit of water as well. The hurdles are special too and not like the ones seen in the 100/110 metres hurdles or the 400-metre hurdles. These do not fall if one collides with them, and in fact, many runners climb on top of the hurdle and try to jump across the water. Whatever the race lacks, it is not variety.

The Martial Art That Is All about Being 'Gentle'

Imagine a sport that revolves around individual combat, and yet, is considered gentle. This is judo. The term 'judo' literally means 'the gentle way' in Japanese. The philosophy of the sport revolves around 'Seiryoku-Zenyo' or 'good use of energy' and 'Jita-Kyoei', which means 'mutual welfare and benefit'. Pretty deep for a sport that is all about throwing people to the ground!

No Pausing Allowed

The pommel horse event in gymnastics is the only event where you can be disqualified for pausing. A pommel horse routine generally lasts between 50–70 seconds, and during this time, the competitor has to be in constant motion. You are not even allowed to hold a pose. Pause and you are out.

The Two Kinds of Racing Cars

While there is a variety of racing cars, experts divide them into two broad categories. These are 'open wheel' and 'closed wheel'. Open-wheel cars have wheels that are outside the car's main body and have room for only one driver, generally seated inside a cockpit-like enclosure. These cars have a very distinct design, low road clearance and are usually not allowed on public roads and have special tracks for them. Formula One cars are an example of open-wheel cars. Closed-wheel cars, on the other hand, have wheels that are inside the car's body and can seat multiple drivers. Their design is closer to normal car design and are allowed to run even on public roads. The NASCAR races are run by closed-wheel cars.

All Cox – the Person in Rowing Who Does Row

In rowing races, every person in a boat uses an oar. The only exception in some cases is the coxswain, also called the cox. The task of the cox is to steer the boat, and when present, they are the only people who can actually see the finish line of the race as they face it (the rowers row with their back to the finish line). The role of the cox is also to control the strategy of the race and take tactical decisions and also to encourage and motivate the rowers.

Poona Is Not Just a Place but a Game… Now Called Badminton!

Poona, a city now known as Pune in western India, was actually the name given to what we now called badminton. The sport of hitting a shuttlecock with racquets was immensely popular in the city, which was then a garrison town with a number of British soldiers. They say the first rules of the game were drawn up in the city in 1873. In fact, the rules of the sport were called the Pune Rules until 1887, when they were changed. The sport was later known as badminton, after Badminton House, the residence of the Duke of Beaufort, although why the sport is so called is still not very clear.

Why Do Long and Triple Jumpers Fall Forward or Sideways?

Anyone who has witnessed long and triple jump events would have observed that athletes almost always fall forwards or sideways after landing in the pit. There is a reason for this – the length of their attempt is measured from the takeoff board to the nearest mark made by athlete's body on landing in the pit. If they end up squatting or even falling backwards, athletes lose distance! Hence the attempts to fall sideways or forwards.

Hockey: The Sport with Multiple Variants

It is doubtful whether any single game has as many popular variants as hockey does. Essentially the same sport – involving using a stick to push an object into the goal – is played on different surfaces with different rules, with different variants being popular in different parts of the world. Some of the variants of hockey are:

- Field hockey – played on grass or turf
- Ice hockey – played on ice (as the name indicates) with skates and with a puck instead of a ball
- Roller hockey – played on normal grass or turf but with the players wearing roller skates
- Rink hockey – played on an indoor surface (generally wooden) with players wearing roller skates
- Floor hockey – played on a smooth surface indoors with players wearing shoes or roller skates

The Two Forms of Rowing

Competitive rowing falls into two very broad categories:

- Sculling: where the rower has two oars, one in each hand.
- Sweeping: where the rower has a single oar, which they grip with both hands.

As a rule, sculls generally go faster than sweeps.

When Royalty Banned Football

England might be considered the birthplace of football, but the sport clearly had a pretty traumatic childhood because it got banned a number of times in that very country. In 1314, King Edward II banned football in London because 'there is great noise in the city caused by hustling over large balls from which many evils may arise which God forbid; we command and forbid, on behalf of the King, on pain of imprisonment, such game to be used in the city in the future'. Edward III and IV banned the sport in England as it was seen as distracting Archery was the go-to cool sport in the Middle Ages. There were other bans too but with limited success, and as we all know, the sport survived and flourished. Whenever England claims 'football is coming home' when they seem likely to win a trophy, we feel like going, 'Yeah, AFTER you banned it so many times!'

Love Tracking Time? Sign up as a Basketball Timekeeper!

Does any sport have as many clocks ticking as basketball? In order to keep the game moving and the action non-stop, there are time constraints on almost everything. For instance:

- When a team gets the ball, it has to get it into their opponents' half within 8 seconds.
- A team has to make an attempt at scoring a basket within 24 seconds of getting the ball
- A player cannot be in a specified area near the basket for more than 3 seconds
- A team can call a timeout of not more than 1 minute and 15 seconds in the middle of a match to discuss strategy.

There are more. The timekeepers are very busy indeed in basketball.

The First International Cricket Match Was NOT between Test-Playing Nations

The first cricket Test match was played between England and Australia at Melbourne in 1877. However, the first cricket match between two nations was played more than thirty years before that, and between two countries that have never played Test cricket. It was played in 1844 between the US and Canada at New York! Interestingly, neither country has ever played a Test match.

The Father of the Football World Cup

There are many who consider the football World Cup (also called the FIFA World Cup) as the most popular sporting event in the world. Well, the tournament did not exist before 1928 and might not have existed even then but for the persistence of one person, Jules Rimet (1873–1956). A lawyer who was immensely interested in football, Rimet was one of the founders of the Fédération Internationale de Football Association (FIFA) in 1904, which is now the body that administers football all over the world. Rimet had a vision of a global football tournament and was involved in the football event in the 1908 Olympic Games. The First World War got in the way of his idea of a 'world cup', but he revived it after he became the president of FIFA in 1921. He announced in 1928 that Uruguay would host the first football World Cup, which was scheduled for 1930. The tournament was a success, and the rest is, as they say, history. Rimet's persistence and ability to convince nations across the world to participate in a tournament earned him the name 'the father of the World Cup'.

In fact, the first edition of the World Cup trophy was named the Jules Rimet Cup in his honour.

Sports with Unlimited Substitutions

Most sports limit the number of substitutes a team can use, but a few literally have no cap on substitutions. Perhaps the most high-profile of these is basketball. Other notable sports that allow unlimited substitutions are hockey, ice hockey, gridiron football and handball. Replacements are never an issue here.

The Mother of Golf!

We have all heard of people being considered as 'fathers' of a sport – Jules Rimet is considered the father of the football World Cup, Baron Pierre de Coubertin is called the father of the modern Olympic Games. Women are generally not accorded such celebrated status as mothers of a sport. An exception is Mary, Queen of Scots (1542–87), who was an enthusiastic golf player and indeed was considered to be the only woman playing the sport in the sixteenth century. So much so that she is called the Mother of Golf.

What Do Those Football Formation Numbers (4-4-2, 3-5-2, 4-3-3, etc.,) Mean?

Most team games that are played with a ball and have a goal generally have team formations that are shown in a set of numbers like 4-4-2 or 3-5-2. What do these numbers mean? Well, in most sports they are used to refer to the number of defending players, middle players (midfield) and advanced players (generally goalscorers). So a 3-5-2 means three defenders, five in the middle and two advanced players. There are variations of this, and some formations have four or even five numbers, but in each case the pattern is the same – the first number is closest to the team's goal and the last number is closest to the goal of the opponent.

The Swimming Champ Who Became the Father of Surfing

Surfing the ocean waves is a very popular hobby and even a full-fledged sport in many countries. The person who made it popular was five-time Olympic gold winner Duke Kahanamoku. A Hawaiian by birth who later became a US citizen, Kahanamoku took surfing, which was largely restricted to Hawaii, to a more global audience by including it in his swimming exhibitions, beginning with a display in California in 1912. Small wonder he is considered the father of surfing.

The Sport in Which Fifteen Nations Participate as One Team

The West Indies cricket team played its first Test match in 1928, before New Zealand, India and Pakistan had. The team also dominated cricket from the 1970s to the early 1990s, won the World Cup in 1975 and 1979 and gave the sport some of its greatest players such as Sir Garfield Sobers and Vivian Richards. The fascinating thing, however, is that there is no country known as the West Indies. West Indies is actually a confederation of fifteen countries and territories in what is called the Caribbean region. Many of these together were known as the British West Indies, which is the root of the name West Indies. These comprise Anguilla, Antigua and Barbuda, Barbados, the British Virgin Islands, Dominica, Grenada, Guyana, Jamaica, Montserrat, St. Kitts and Nevis, St. Lucia, St. Maarten, St. Vincent and the

Grenadines, Trinidad and Tobago and the United States Virgin Islands. This is a very rare phenomenon in sport. Countries do come together to play as a single team but only for specific tournaments – say for matches between continents. The West Indies, however, is a group of nations that has always played every kind of cricket match. In fact, the domestic cricket tournament of the West Indies, called the Shell Shield, is actually an international one as it is contested by teams that would, in other sports, have been representing nations (Jamaica, Guyana, Trinidad and Tobago and so on).

The Sport Where Play Keeps Stopping

Imagine a sport where play is stopped every ten minutes to enable the teams to take a break? Well, that is basketball. Basketball matches are generally forty or forty-eight minutes in duration and are divided into four quarters of ten or twelve minutes each. There are breaks after each period (each team is allowed seven timeouts – small intervals in play – each) and a halftime break of about a quarter of an hour too. There are also breaks of play and timeouts. Some people say that basketball is the most interrupted sport of them all, with breaks and intervals taking up more time than the actual game.

The Man Who Invented Rugby

It is rare to find a sport being credited to a single person, but such is the case with rugby football, also simply called rugby. There is a very popular belief that the game was invented during a football match at Rugby School in the UK in 1823. As this was a football match, players were not allowed to touch the ball with their hands. However, in the course of this particular match, a seventeen-year-old student called William Webb Ellis picked up the football and ran with it. Legend has it that this created rugby football, which is a blend of kicking and carrying the ball. While many historians contest this version, William Webb Ellis is widely credited with creating the sport of rugby, and even the trophy of the Rugby World Cup is called the Webb Ellis Cup.

They Were Looking for a Sport Less Injury Prone than Football… And Basketball Was Born

It is one of the most popular sports in the world today (and particularly in the US), but basketball actually owes its origins to football. Sort of. The game was conceived in 1891 by James Naismith (1861–1939), a physical education instructor at what is now known as the Springfield College in Massachusetts. He came up with the sport to keep athletes fit while staying indoors in winter months. He used peach baskets nailed near the gym balcony and asked players to throw the ball into them. Contact was limited, and tackling and pushing were not allowed.

Types of Balls in Sports

Why Runners Start at Different Points in Some Races

In many races (generally up to 400 metres and sometimes in the 800 metres, excluding the 100 metres), it is observed that the runners start from different parts of the track. This is called a staggered start and is done to ensure that all runners end up running the same distance. If this was not done, the runners in the outside lanes would end up running more than those in the inside lanes in an oval-shaped track. There is no staggering in 100 metres as it is run in a straight line. In races more than 400 metres, runners are allowed to switch lanes.

The Man Who Designed Modern Tennis

While tennis was being played in some form or the other since medieval times, the credit for inventing modern tennis – tennis in its current form – is given to Major Walter Clopton Wingfield (1833–1912). He is believed to have come up with the idea of using vulcanized rubber balls and also using croquet lawns for playing it, which led to its being called 'lawn tennis'. Wingfield actually patented his style of the sport and sold equipment in boxed sets that contained balls, rackets, court markers and even nets and poles, from which the game we play today can be seen to have evolved. The Wimbledon Lawn Tennis Museum features a bust of Wingfield for his contributions.

Why Are Basketball Baskets Open?

Ever wondered why the baskets used in basketball matches are always kept open at the base? Well, it is for purely functional reasons. Initial games of basketball played in the 1890s were played with proper fruit baskets placed at a height. The problem with these was that the game had to be stopped every time a team scored a basket as someone had to climb up and retrieve the ball. The players finally figured that it made more sense to remove the lower parts of the baskets so that the ball could bounce right out and back into the playing area.

The Caddie Story in Golf

One of the hallmarks of a golf tournament are the caddies, people who walk with players, carry their clubs and often advise them about which club to choose. Most players have their own dedicated caddies who travel with them across the world for tournaments. But when did the whole concept of caddie come into being, and why are they called 'caddies' instead of something more routine, like 'assistants'? Well, according to many, the credit for this goes to the person known as the Mother of Golf, Mary, Queen of Scots, perhaps the first and only woman to play golf in the sixteenth century. Being royalty, she did not carry her own golf clubs. Her clubs were carried by army cadets. It is believed that the word 'caddie' has actually been derived from 'cadet'!

The Race Inspired by Racing from One Church to Another

For many people, the 3,000 metres steeplechase looks like a very odd race. The runners not only have to run on the track but also jump over hurdles and even pass a water barrier. Why is this race in this form and why is it called a 'steeplechase'? Well, that is because it is inspired by races in the UK in the nineteenth century where people raced each other from one church to another. As only the churches' steeples were visible from a distance, the race was soon being called a race to the steeple, from which the term 'steeplechase' comes. Also, as the running was done in country conditions and not on the track, runners often had to encounter all kinds of obstacles, including bushes, walls and water. It is this that the 3,000-metre steeplechase tries to emulate on a track!

Swimming? You Cannot Stay Underwater for More Than 15 seconds

In most swimming competitions, you have to spend most of the time with your head above the surface of the water. Your head has to break the surface within 15 metres of touching the wall, whether from the start or on the turn. The only event to which this does not apply is in the breaststroke.

Birdie, Eagle, Albatross – Golf's Obsession with Birds!

The aim in golf is to put the ball in the hole in a certain number of strokes. The number of strokes is worked out in advance and is called 'par'. If a person places the ball in the hole in one stroke lesser than the par number, he is supposed to have scored a 'birdie'. If he does so in two strokes less than par, he is said to have scored an 'eagle'. Three strokes under par are termed an 'albatross' or a 'double eagle'. Why this obsession with bird names for golf scores? Well, it is evidently because in the early days of the sport, a good shot was applauded as 'a bird of a shot'! ('Bird' is US slang for 'good'). Over par scores, incidentally, have no bird affiliations. They are simply called 'bogeys', and are believed to be derived from the Scottish term 'bogle' or the English 'bogey man', a sort of devil. 'Par' is believed to have come from the stock exchange, where a share was said to be trading above or below its 'par' price.

Any Space Will Do: The Sport with No Standardized Playing Area!

Most sports are played in well-defined (or at least loosely defined) playing areas, with specific dimensions. Golf is an exception. The sport has literally no set dimensions (except for the hole, which has to be four inches deep and 4.25 inches in diameter), and even the terrain is different on different golf courses around the world. You could have forests at one place and none at another. This is why winning in golf is very difficult.

Get Your Rackets in the Right Colours, Please

Table tennis rackets, or 'paddles' as some term them, have to adhere to a strict colour code. They are generally made of wood and come with rubber on both sides. However, the texture of the rubber on each side could be different – it could be thicker to help spin, for instance. This is why the regulations of the game insist that not only do both sides of a table tennis racket have different colours but even specify them – one side of a table tennis racket has to be black, while the other can be red, blue, pink, violet or green. Players can inspect each other's rackets before a match to find out which side is designed for which style of play.

The Different Heights of Hurdles

Athletics tournaments generally feature two hurdles events each for men and women – 110 metres hurdles and 400 metres hurdles for the men, and 100 metres hurdles and 400 metres hurdles for women. While the hurdles are present in all these events and are ten in number in each race, their heights are different. The hurdles used in the men's 110 metres hurdles are 1.067 metres tall, while those used in the women's 100 metres hurdles are 0.8 metres high. Similarly, in the 400 metres hurdles, the men have to leap over 0.914 metres high hurdles, while the women have to cross hurdles that are 0.762 metres tall!

Gymnastics and Gender: VERY Different for Men and Women

In most sports, men and women tend to contest broadly similar events, with differences mainly in terms of distances and weights involved. Gymnastics is an exception to this. In gymnastics, men and women generally compete in very different events with radically different equipment and accessories. Only two disciplines – the floor exercise and the vault – are contested by both genders. Women have two exclusive events – the beam and the uneven bars. Men have four exclusive events – pommel horse, rings, uneven bars and the parallel bars.

Rowing? You Won't Be Able to See the Finish Line!

Imagine a race in which almost none of the participants can see the finish line? Well, that is what happens in rowing, where contestants almost always row with their back to the finish line. They normally judge the distance travelled by the number of strokes they make or are guided by a coxswain (cox), who is a pilot of sorts allowed in some boats! This is why a lot of stress is placed on getting into the lead as soon as possible. The reason for this is simple: most rowers have their backs to the finishing line, so they actually have no idea of how far a boat is ahead of them – they can only monitor the boats next to them or behind them. So, in rowing, getting ahead is the best way of staying ahead.

The Combat Sport Where Both Players Wear the Same Colour!

When two teams or individuals play each other in a sport that involves contact, they generally wear different colours to enable the officials to distinguish between them easily. A very notable exception to this is judo, in which both contestants are supposed to dress in similar snow-white robes. The confusion caused by this has led to the introduction of suits of contrasting colours in a number of tournaments. In the land of its birth, Japan, however, judo is still contested by opponents dressed in white, with one wearing a red belt to distinguish them from the other!

Ballet and Fencing – a Fascinating Relationship!

Ballet is one of the most elegant dance forms in the world, aesthetically pleasing and requiring a lot of skill and patience. According to many, the dance form, which developed in the fifteenth century, was actually a dance interpretation of the sport of fencing. Louis XIV of France, a keen fencer himself, is believed to have played a key rule in its development in the seventeenth century. Many historians have noted the similarity of postures adopted in both ballet and fencing, and while there is no conclusive evidence of ballet having emerged from fencing, it certainly does seem to have been influenced by it.

The Different Formats of Cricket

Cricket is played in three formats at the international level:

1. Test Cricket: Teams play each other over a period of four or five days.

2. One-Day Internationals (ODIs): Each team plays the same number of overs (generally 50) on the same day.
3. T20 Internationals: Each team plays 20 overs each.

Rugby Union vs Rugby League

Mention the word 'rugby', and some folks might be confused if you are referring to rugby union or rugby league. Both sports are broadly similar in terms of your having to carry a ball over a line or to score a goal. They have, however, different regulations and scoring systems. The most significant difference between the two sports is that rugby league is played with 13 players while rugby union is played with 15. Only seven substitutions are allowed during a game of rugby union, while ten are allowed in a rugby league match.

The Bird behind Badminton

There would be no badminton without geese. The game consists of players hitting a shuttlecock across a net. This shuttlecock has a base of cork with feathers embedded in it. While these feathers are sometimes made of plastic, generally they come from a goose. Each shuttlecock has sixteen goose feathers in it. Why sixteen? Because evidently, this was the perfect number for flight and spin, as determined by a number of tests.

A Game Was Never as 'Alive' as This

Mughal emperor Akbar (1542–1605) loved playing pachisi, an Indian variant of chess. However, he added a really 'live' element to it by using human beings as pieces on the board, particularly when he played the game at his court at Fatehpur Sikri.

No Legs and Feet, Please; I Am a Pommel Horse!

The pommel horse is very unique in gymnastics – gymnasts are not allowed to touch it with their legs or their feet and can use only their hands to touch it while performing their routines.

The Fastest Racket Sport

Tennis and table tennis are played at high speed, and so is squash, but if you are looking for the fastest racket sport in the world, it is actually badminton. Shuttles can go at speeds of more than 300 kmph – a tennis serve is generally about 200 kmph.

Why Is a Shuttlecock Called a Shuttlecock?

The shuttlecock in badminton gets its name from the shuttle of a loom, which also goes back and forth just like a shuttlecock does in a match of badminton. The 'cock' comes from the feathers, which reminded some early players of a rooster.

The Only Swimming Races That Start in the Pool (Most Start Outside!)

In almost all swimming races, the participants stand outside the pool and jump into it at the start. However, there are two exceptions to this – the backstroke and the medley races, where the racers start from the pool itself, holding on to the wall and then launching themselves backwards into the water.

That Complicated Table Tennis Serve

Serving in almost all sports, such as tennis and badminton, has its own set of rules, but when it comes to table tennis, the serve is tied with a truckload of rules. Here's what someone serving in table tennis needs to keep in mind:

a. They have to stand behind the end line on the table.
b. They cannot toss the ball above or hit it over the playing area (the table).
c. They have to hold the ball above the height of the table.
d. They have to make sure their opponent can see the ball.
e. The ball has to be in the palm of their hand and the palm has to be completely open.
f. They cannot spin the ball while throwing it in the air to serve.
g. The ball has to be thrown at least 16 cm in the air.
h. The throw has to be 'almost vertical'.
i. They can strike the ball only when it is on its way down.
j. The ball has to bounce on the server's side of the table and once on the side across the net.

Did the Chinese Invent Football?

Football, the world's most popular sport, might have originated in China. The earliest reference to a game in which a ball is kicked comes from China, where in the third century BCE, cuju was very popular. Cuju literally means 'kick ball' and involved kicking a ball into a net without using one's hands. It became very popular in the era of the Han dynasty.

Got the Ball? You Can Only Move Three Steps, and Have Only Three Seconds

Once you get the ball in handball, you can only take a maximum of three steps before you pass it or dribble it past someone by bouncing it. What's more, if you have the ball and stop moving, you have three seconds to either shoot or pass the ball or try to dribble past an opponent.

The Power of Glue in Table Tennis

One of the fascinating aspects of table tennis is the fact that the glue used to stick the rubber surface to the racket or paddle was once a major factor in performance. This was discovered in the 1970s when a table tennis player used bicycle puncture repair glue to repair his table tennis racket.The difference in performance was so dramatic that players started using the glue, often preparing their rackets half an hour before a match. The glue was called speed glue and was in widespread use before finally being banned in 2008 due to health concerns.

Table Tennis Is Bad for the Eyes? Ask the Soviets

It is said that table tennis was banned in the erstwhile USSR from 1930 to 1950. The reason? It was believed to be bad for the eyes!

The Lightest Ball in Sport? It Is Found on a Table

While there are a number of ball sports in the world, the lightest ball of them all is used in table tennis. A table tennis ball is a mere 2.7 grams in weight.

The Two Forms of Wrestling

Wrestling is one of the oldest sports in the world and was even a part of the ancient Olympic Games. In its modern avatar, wrestling comes in two forms – Greco-Roman wrestling, where the wrestlers can only use their arms and upper body, and freestyle wrestling, where the wrestlers can use their arms as well as their legs to pin their opponents.

The Man Who Added a Third Stump to a Wicket in Cricket

In cricket, the aim of the bowler is to hit the wicket, which is a set of three stumps with bails on top. In the early days of the game, there were only two stumps in the wicket. That changed in 1775 when Edward 'Lumpy' Stevens, considered by many to be the first truly great bowler in the sport, beat a batsman called John Small three times, only for the ball to go between the two stumps. There are many who believe that it was this event that led to a third stump being added to a cricket wicket.

The Game That Started from Prison

One of the healthiest sports in the world owes its origins to prison. Prisoners in London's famous Fleet Prison used to play a game that involved hitting the ball against the walls with a racket. The game itself was called 'rackets'. It is believed that students of Harrow School picked up the game and made the ball a punctured rubber one to add more variety. The punctured ball would get 'squashed' against the wall again and again as the players ran around to keep it in play. The sport is now known as the intense and extremely hectic squash!

Why Is Tennis Called... Tennis?

Many believe that the word 'tennis' is actually derived from the French word 'tenez.' The word means 'take this' and was evidently shouted by players in France in the early days of the sport whenever they struck the ball!

Those Lanes in Athletics? You Do Not Always Need to Run in Them

Athletics tracks come with clearly marked lanes for different runners. However, athletes do not always have to stay strictly within those lanes. Athletes cannot move out of their lanes in sprint events but can move out in middle and long distance events (sometimes after a certain distance has been covered). Which is why, in most middle and long distance events, you find most athletes ending up running in the innermost lane, which is actually the shortest!

The Athletics Event Where Women Seem to Do Better Than Men

In all athletics events, men run (and walk) faster and throw, leap and jump further than women. With one exception. When it comes to the discus throw, women generally throw the discus further than their male counterparts. At the time of writing, the world record in the discus throw for men stood at 74.08 metres (by Jurgen Schult in 1986), while the record for women was more than 2 metres ahead of this at 76.80 metres in the name of Gabriele Reinsch (1988). The reason for this is simple – the women's discus is half the weight of a men's discus – 1 kilogram as compared to 2 kilograms. The discus used for men is also larger, with a diameter of 22 centimetres. The discus for women is 18 centimetres in diameter. Interestingly, this 'women throwing further than men' phenomenon is not seen in other throwing events (shot-put, javelin throw and hammer throw) even though women get lighter and smaller items to throw in those events as well.

Kayaks, Canoes – What's the Row about the Difference?

They are both boats used in Olympic rowing sports, they look similar, and those in them use paddles to drive and steer them. So what is the difference between a canoe and a kayak? Well, the paddler in a kayak is actually seated and uses a double-bladed paddle. On the other hand, the paddler in a canoe either sits or kneels and uses a single-bladed paddle. Canoes are also more open in terms of design, while occupants of kayaks are almost 'sealed' into their positions. Kayaks are generally lighter and also move faster than canoes.

The Duck and Zero!

In many sports (most notably cricket), the number zero is called a 'duck'. The reason for this is incredibly simple – the shape of zero is similar to a duck's egg!

Badminton Played with the Feet?

Imagine hitting a shuttlecock across a badminton court, not with a racket but your foot! That is actually a sport called jianzi. It is played on badminton courts and even in the open with just a line separating the players instead of the net. The shuttlecock is slightly different from badminton, though, with feathers stuck on a disc-shaped base. The sport is actually also called shuttlecock and featherball.

To Find Out More about the Ball, Look at the Dots

The ball used in the sport of squash is generally dark but can come in other colours too. What's more, each ball has different coloured dots on them. Contrary to what many think, these are not for design or appearance but actually refer to the speed and bounce of the ball. A pair of yellow dots (double yellow) indicates an extra super slow ball, a single yellow dot indicates a super slow ball, a green or white dot means a slow ball, a red dot refers to a medium fast ball, and finally, a blue dot indicates a fast ball. The yellow and double yellow dot balls are used for professional level competitions, and beginners are encouraged to start with the blue dot ball.

Only Three Touches of the Ball Allowed

In volleyball, a team can touch a ball only three times before sending it across the net. Any more, and they lose the point.

Cricket Was a Part of the First Modern Olympics

Cricket is all set to be an Olympic sport in the 2028 edition as per some reports. However, the sport has not had a very happy history in the Olympics. It made its only full appearance in the 1904 Games, where only two teams competed: Great Britain, which beat France for the gold. Interestingly, cricket was supposed to have been a part of the first modern Olympic Games in 1896, but the event could not be held for a very odd reason – there were not enough teams!

The Player with a Different-Coloured Jersey on a Volleyball Court

In volleyball, most players belonging to a team wear the same colours. There is one exception, though. This is of a player labelled as libero. The libero is a specialized defensive player and cannot make an attack hit. It is not compulsory for a team to play a libero, but most teams do at some stage.

The Race in Which Contestants Start Moving before the Starting Line

Most races get underway with the contestants starting from a still position (also called a 'standing' position) from the starting line. There are a few exceptions, though. The most notable is sailing, in which the boats are already moving by the time they approach the starting point. In fact, ensuring that you hit the starting point at just the right speed is a vital part of sailing.

Lose Weight: It Helps in… Weightlifting

Weightlifting is not just about lifting weight but also keeping your own self relatively light. If two weightlifters end up lifting the same weight, then the one with the lower body weight is often declared the winner.

The Statue That Launched the Modern Olympics

In 1896, the first modern Olympic Games were held at Athens. It was the first time that the Olympics had been held since ancient times. And they started with the unveiling of a statue. It was the statue of a Greek without whom the Games would not have been possible. No, it was not some legendary athlete or God. It was a statue of Georgios Averoff, a Greek businessman and philanthropist, who had contributed significant sums of money for the event.

Statue of Georgios Averoff, Athens, Greece

CHAPTER TWO

Great Tournaments and Arenas

Why is a Stadium Called… A Stadium? The Reason Is Race-Ist!

Sports arenas are called stadiums for a simple reason. In ancient times, the most watched event was a 190-metre foot race called the stade. It was run on sand in an open area. As people started to gather to watch it, people began building seating spaces around it for them to sit. And before you knew it, you had large places with a single track in the middle for the stade race. Not surprisingly, the places where the stade was run in front of large crowds began to be called 'stadiums' or 'stadia'.

Marching Past at the Olympics – the Countries Are Always First and Last

Every Olympic Games starts with an opening ceremony featuring a march past of the athletes participating in the Games. The order of the countries in this march past is always alphabetical, with two exceptions – Greece is always the first country, being the birthplace of the Games, and the host nation is always the last country.

The Oldest Sports Trophy of Them All

Today, it is routine to see a trophy being awarded to the winner of a competition. However, this was not the case in the initial years of sport. In the ancient Olympics, winners were given wreaths made of leaves and sometimes jars of olive oil. Slowly, other objects such as vases, weapons (shields in particular) and cups began to make an appearance. The oldest trophy in sport as per most sources is a pair of bells that is given to the winner of the prestigious Carlisle Bell horse race in the UK. This was first awarded in 1599 by Queen Elizabeth I!

The Tournament with Grass That Is Cut to an Exact Height

Wimbledon is the world's most prestigious tennis tournament. It is one of the few grass court tournaments left in the world and takes a lot of care of its grass. The grass at Wimbledon is mowed to an exact height of 8 mm and is rolled carefully. Players have to wear shoes with rubber soles to minimize damage to the grass.

The Olympics between the Ancient and Modern Olympics

Mention the Olympics, and most people will think that you are either referring to the ancient Olympics that started in 776 BCE in Greece or the modern ones pioneered by Baron Pierre de Coubertin in 1896. There were, however, a sort of Olympic Games in between these two. With a slightly different spelling, though. These were the Cotswold Olympick Games held in Chipping, Campdale, in England. They started in 1612 and were the initiative of a lawyer named Robert Dover. They had the support of King James I, and over the years, featured events like running, jumping, dancing, sledgehammer throwing, horse racing, coursing with hounds, sword and cudgel fighting, wrestling and even shin-kicking. They were very irregularly hosted but were reasonably popular among different classes of society. They were finally totally discontinued in 1862. They were semi-revived in 1963 and have been taking place off and on ever since. They might have been rather local, but their format and duration has led to them being called 'the first stirrings of Britain's Olympic beginnings' by the British Olympic Association. Oh, and their spelling remains unchanged.

The Story of the Olympic Torch in the Modern Olympics (Hitler Did Have a Role)

One of the most stirring sights of any Olympic Games is the torch relay where different runners carry the Olympic torch culminating in the lighting of the Olympic flame. However, there was no torch relay in the modern Olympic Games for quite some time, although the Olympic flame was introduced in 1928. The torch relay was first featured in the 1936 Olympic Games and is believed to have been conceived by Dr Carl Diem of Germany. The relay started from Olympia, the home of the ancient Olympics, and passed through seven countries before ending in the stadium to get the games underway. The first man to carry the flame was Konstantin Kondylis of Greece, and the honour of carrying it into the stadium was entrusted to Fritz Schilgen of Germany (who it is said was picked because he had an attractive running style – such things mattered in Hitler's Germany).

The Home of Golf

St. Andrews Links, located in the Scottish town of St. Andrews, is considered to be the home of golf. This is because golf is believed to have started there in the fourteenth century. Indeed, it got so popular that King James II of Scotland banned the sport in 1457 as it distracted the youth from archery. King James III upheld the ban, and who knows what would have happened to St. Andrews in particular and golf in general if King James IV had not turned out to be a golfer himself. He retracted the ban in 1502, and when, fifty years later, the Archbishop himself gave the townspeople the right to play on the links, golf had found its home.

The Race Where Coming First Does Not Matter

In most races, getting to the finish line before your competitors is what determines the winner. But not in the case of the legendary 24 Hours of Le Mans sports car race. The race is totally endurance based, and as its name indicates, runs for 24 hours non-stop. The car that covers the greatest distance in this period of time is declared the winner. This is quite a test for the cars as they have not only got to keep running for 24 hours but also cover a fair amount of distance. The record distance covered in the race is 5,410 kilometres or about 3,360 miles. For context, that's about 18 times the distance of a Formula One Grand Prix.

The Olympic Games That Took Place after Two Years!

The modern Olympic Games were supposed to be held every four years, just as their ancient counterparts. However, the first Olympic Games in 1896 were such a huge success that in 1900, a proposal was put forward to have two types of Olympic Games – one which would would be hosted by different cities all over the world and one which would be always hosted by Greece, the home of the original Olympics. Each of these would follow a four-year cycle but would be two years apart. So the world would have Olympic Games every two years. The first of these Games was held in 1906 in Athens. They were a huge success, but disturbances in Greece made it impossible for the next edition of these Games to be hosted in 1910. The First World War prevented the 1914 Games from taking place, and by the time the war was over, interest in the Games had all but vanished. The 1906 Games are referred to as the Intercalated Games by some experts, and some observers refuse to consider them as 'proper' Olympic Games, although they were recognized by the IOC, which was responsible for organizing the Olympic Games.

The Olympics with No Closing Ceremony

The closing ceremony is one of the most important events of an Olympics. However, the second modern Olympic Games in 1900 at Paris were so poorly organized (they spanned over five months, and many athletes did not even know they were competing or had won in the Olympics) that they actually ended without a proper closing ceremony.

The Most Crowded Sports Trophy in the World!

It is common to have the name of the winning player or team engraved on a trophy. But imagine a trophy that has not just the name of the winning team but also the names of the players and its coaches, management and staff engraved on it! Well, the Stanley Cup, the most prestigious trophy in ice hockey, does just that. Which is why the original cup actually sits on top of rows of circles that contain the names of the winners. New rings are added and old ones removed. As of now, there are more than two thousand names on that trophy!

Cities That Have Hosted the Olympic Games

Year	Host City, Country
1896	Athens, Greece
1900	Paris, France

1904	St. Louis, US
1906	Athens, Greece
1908	London, England, UK
1912	Stockholm, Sweden
1916	Berlin, Germany (cancelled, because of World War I)
1920	Antwerp, Belgium
1924	Paris, France
1928	Amsterdam, The Netherlands
1932	Los Angeles, US
1936	Berlin, Germany
1940	Tokyo, Japan/Helsinki, Finland (cancelled, because of World War II)
1944	London, England, UK (cancelled, because of World War II)
1948	London, England, UK
1952	Helsinki, Finland
1956	Melbourne, Australia
1960	Rome, Italy
1964	Tokyo, Japan
1968	Mexico City, Mexico
1972	Munich, Germany
1976	Montreal, Canada
1980	Moscow, USSR
1984	Los Angeles, US
1988	Seoul, South Korea
1992	Barcelona, Spain
1996	Atlanta, US
2000	Sydney, Australia
2004	Athens, Greece
2008	Beijing, China
2012	London, England, UK
2016	Rio, Brazil

2021	Tokyo, Japan (delayed because of COVID)
2024	Paris, France
2028	Los Angeles, US
2032	Brisbane, Australia

The Continent That Has Never Hosted the Olympics

By some odd coincidence (and maybe a combination of money and politics), no Olympic Games have ever been hosted in Africa. In fact, the Games had never been to South America either and were first seen in that continent in 2016 when Rio in Brazil hosted the Olympics.

Why is Cricket's Most Famous Ground Called 'Lord's'?

Cricket has some very famous grounds like the Eden Gardens in Kolkata and the MCG at Melbourne. However, its most famous playing field is Lord's in London, which is also referred to as the 'Home of Cricket'. Not too many know why the ground is called Lord's, and some even think it has something to do with a title of Lord. The truth is much simpler – the ground originally belonged to Thomas Lord. It was 'Lord's ground'. It has since been acquired by the Marylebone Cricket Club (MCC) but is still referred to as Lord's.

The Olympics Did Not Have Gold, Silver and Bronze Medals for a While

The winner of an Olympic event is normally given a gold medal, the runner-up gets a silver medal and the third placed player or team a bronze medal. But this was not the case for quite a while. Winners in the 1896 Olympic Games were given a silver medal and a wreath made of an olive branch, while the runner-up got a wreath made of laurel and a copper or bronze medal. The 1900 Olympics put another spin on design, with some winners receiving medals (which were rectangular) and some receiving cups and other trophies. The whole concept of gold, silver and bronze medals was introduced in the 1904 Olympics at St. Louis, and has stayed with us ever since.

The First Athlete to Light the Olympic Torch

One of the most important parts of the opening ceremony of any Olympic Games is the lighting of the Olympic flame, which burns for the duration of the Games. This torch is normally lit by a well-known athlete or personality. This was not always the case. The concept of the torch and flame was introduced in the 1936 Olympic Games, and it was carried forward in the 1948 Games too. However, in both these cases, the person lighting the flame (or cauldron, as some refer to it) was not a competitor and was picked for their appearance. It was only in 1952 that the role was given to a well-known athlete, with Finland's legendary Paavo Nurmi lighting the flame!

The Secret in Every Olympic Opening Ceremony

The opening ceremony of every Olympic Games is an elaborate and carefully arranged event. Schedules and programmes are prepared and sent out in advance. One detail of the opening ceremony is, however, almost never revealed. This is the identity of the person who will light the Olympic flame. It is a secret that is very carefully kept, ensuring an element of surprise when the person finally emerges.

Swearing at the Olympics: The Introduction of the Olympic Flag and Oath

The carrying of the Olympic flag and the taking of the Olympic oath are an integral part of the opening ceremony of the Olympics. However, this tradition was started in the 1920 Olympic Games at Antwerp. Victor Boin of Belgium, the host country, took the oath on behalf of his athletes.

What Are Those Rings in the Olympic Symbol For?

The Olympic symbol is of five interlaced rings of equal size. The rings are differently coloured and are blue, yellow, black, green and red. It was designed by Baron Pierre de Coubertin (the father of the modern Olympics) and was first displayed in 1913. The rings represent the five continents and the meeting of their athletes at the Olympic Games. Coubertin also included the white background of the rings in the colour list and famously said that 'the six colors thus combined reproduce those of all nations without exception'.

The Three-Word Olympic Motto That Got a Fourth Word Later on

The original Olympic oath comprised three words in Latin – 'Citius – Altius – Fortius'. These mean 'Faster – Higher – Stronger' and are believed to have been uttered by Henri Didon, a Dominican priest, at the opening ceremony of a school sports event in 1881. Among the audience was Pierre de Coubertin, who would go on to revive the Olympic Games. He adopted the three words as the Olympic motto in 1894, and it was first used in the 1924 Olympics. In 2021, the IOC added the word

'Communiter' (Together) after an en-dash following these three words. So the current Olympic motto is – 'Citius, Altius, Fortius – Communiter' or 'Faster, Higher, Stronger – Together'.

Women Had a Cricket World Cup before the Men Did

Women's cricket was often ignored by the authorities and administrators, with men's cricket getting more attention and investments. That said, women had a World Cup well before their male counterparts did. The first women's World Cup was held in 1973, a full two years before the first men's World Cup.

Badminton's Oldest and Greatest Tournament

The most prestigious tournament in badminton is not the World Championships or the Olympics but the All England Open Badminton Champions, also called the All England. It is also the sport's oldest tournament, having been first played all the way back in 1898.

The World Cup with No Final

The final is considered to be the centre stage of any sports tournament, deciding the winner of the event. And the football World Cup final has been one of the most watched events over the years, with tickets being sold in advance for it. It is therefore remarkable that the 1950 World Cup in Brazil actually had no final. The organizers came up with a format where the winner would be decided from a group of four teams who would play each other, with the team getting the most points being declared the winner. There was no designated 'final' match to decide the winner. By some coincidence, though, the last match in this group was between the two teams who were topping the group – Brazil and Uruguay. Brazil needed a draw to win the tournament, Uruguay needed to win. Uruguay won 2–1, and the match is remembered by many as the final as it was the last match of the tournament and did decide the winner. The truth, however, is that it was a group match!

The Most Prestigious Ice Hockey Trophy Does Not Have Its Own Name on It!

One of the most famous trophies in sport is the Stanley Cup, which is awarded to the winner of the National Hockey League ice hockey championship, and is one of the oldest trophies in North America, going all the way back to 1893. The odd thing is that the words 'Stanley Cup' do not appear anywhere on the trophy itself. So why is it called the Stanley Cup? Well, it is believed that this is because the trophy was donated by Lord Frederick Stanley, who was the governor general of Canada in 1892. He gave it to be awarded to the best amateur ice hockey club in Canada. It is officially called the Dominion Hockey Challenge Cup, but everyone knows it as the Stanley Cup!

The Olympics That Are Credited to Two Host Countries… But Were Never Held

The 1940 Olympic Games have a unique place in history. They are the only Olympic Games to have been credited to two different countries – Tokyo in Japan and Helsinki in Finland. What had happened was that the 1940 Games were originally awarded to Tokyo in 1932. However, the outbreak of the Sino-Japanese war in 1937 led to Japan forfeiting the right to host the Games in 1938. The Games were then awarded to Helsinki, which had been the runner-up to Tokyo in the original bidding process. However, these too had to be cancelled when World War II broke out.

Olympics? No Women Allowed

Women were not allowed to participate in not just the ancient Olympic Games but even in the first modern Olympics held at Athens in 1896. Although there were some events for women in ancient Greece, these were not considered part of the Olympics. In fact, as per some sources, women were not even permitted in the Games as spectators, although there is some confusion in this regard – a few scribes claim that married women were not allowed to attend events. When the Olympic Games were revived in 1896 at Athens, they were without any women competitors. Women competed for the first time in the modern Olympics – perhaps for the first time in Olympic history – in the 1900 Games at Paris. Women were allowed to participate alongside men in sailing and croquet and also had their own individual contests in tennis and golf.

No Football At the Olympics? Blame It on the World Cup

Football has always been a part of the Olympic Games since its first appearance in the 1900 Games. However, it was left out of the 1932 Olympics at Los Angeles as FIFA, the organizaton administering the sport at the global level, asked for it to be excluded from the Games to promote its own World Cup, which had started in 1930.

Four Sports That Have Always Been in the Olympics

The Olympic Games have a number of sports in them. The first Olympic Games in 1896 had nine sports, and the 2024 Games at Paris will have 32 sports. Every Olympics sees a number of sports being added or removed. However, four sports have always been a part of the Olympic Games, in some form or the other, right from 1896:

Athletics (track and field)
Swimming
Gymnastics
Fencing

The First Olympics with a Parade of Nations... Was Not an Olympics

The opening of an Olympics is marked by a parade of the athletes under their national banners. However, this did not take place in most of the early Olympics and was first seen only in the 1906 Olympic Games (the intermediary games), which many do not consider to be proper Olympics. The custom was carried over to the official Games afterwards and was seen in the 1908 Games at London.

Tennis's Four Great Tournaments

Tennis has four very prestigious titles – the French Open, Wimbledon, the US Open and the Australian Open. These are played at different times of the year – the Australian Open in January, the French Open in May–June, Wimbledon in June–July and the US Open in August–September. The first Wimbledon tournament was played in 1877, the first US Open in 1881, the first French Open in 1891 and the first Australian Open in 1905.

Tennis's Greatest Tournament Is Known by Its Location

Ask any person who follows tennis about the most prestigious tournament in the sport, and it is a fair chance that he or she will reply, 'Wimbledon'. However, while everyone knows the tournament as 'Wimbledon', its actual name is 'The Championships, Wimbledon'. Interestingly, it is the only one of the four tennis Grand Slam tournaments to be known by its venue!

Tennis's Greatest Tournament is the Only Major Tournament Played on Grass

Many still refer to 'tennis' as 'lawn tennis'. This is because tennis was largely played on grass in its early years, although some also played it on clay. However, with the passage of time, the sport moved to artificial surfaces made of different materials ranging from concrete to Rebound Ace as these were less affected by the weather and easier to maintain. Today, only one major tennis tournament is played on grass. Mind you, it is the most prestigious tournament of them all – Wimbledon.

Grand Slam Tournaments of Tennis

Hosts of the Football World Cup

The football World Cup, also referred to as the FIFA World Cup, is considered to be the most popular sporting event in the world.

The tournament was started in 1930 and has been (and will be) hosted by the following countries:

1930: Uruguay
1934: Italy
1938: France
1950: Brazil
1954: Switzerland
1958: Sweden
1962: Chile
1966: England
1970: Mexico
1974: West Germany
1978: Argentina
1982: Spain
1986: Mexico
1990: Italy
1994: United States
1998: France
2002: Japan and South Korea
2006: Germany
2010: South Africa
2014: Brazil
2018: Russia
2022: Qatar
2026: Canada, Mexico and the United States

Hosts of the Cricket World Cup

The first cricket World Cup (now also known as the ICC World Cup) was held in 1975, and since then, has been contested roughly every four years. It is one of the most popular sporting events in the world as it is followed by some of the most populous nations. These have been the nations that have hosted the cricket World Cup down the years and will host some of the forthcoming editions:

1975	England
1979	England
1983	England
1987	India and Pakistan
1992	Australia and New Zealand
1996	India, Pakistan, Sri Lanka
1999	England
2003	South Africa, Zimbabwe, Kenya
2007	West Indies
2011	India, Sri Lanka, Bangladesh
2015	Australia and New Zealand
2019	England and Wales
2023	India
2027	South Africa, Zimbabwe, Namibia
2031	India and Bangladesh

The Tournament with Frequent Multi-Nation Hosts

Most major tournaments are hosted by a single country, or at the most, by two (often neighbouring) countries. The cricket World Cup has, however, been an exception to this. The tournament has been hosted by three nations three times: India, Pakistan and Sri Lanka in 1996; South Africa, Zimbabwe and Kenya in 2003; and India, Sri Lanka and Bangladesh in 2011. It has also been hosted by two nations four times: India and Pakistan in 1987; Australia and New Zealand in 1992 and 2015; and England and Wales in 2019. This multi-national hosting tendency is set to continue in the coming years – the 2027 World Cup is to be hosted by South Africa, Zimbabwe and Namibia while India and Bangladesh will host the 2031 World Cup.

Why Are Sports Tournaments Called 'Open'?

It is common to see a number of tournaments come with the word 'Open' associated with them – the US Open, the Italian Open, the French Open and so on. The term is generally used to indicate that a tournament is 'open' to entry to all players. This might sound a little obvious today, but there were initially restrictions on who could play a certain tournament. For instance, in tennis, professionals were not allowed to compete in many tournaments until 1968, when the 'Open era' is believed to have started. Similarly, the French Clay Court Championships were renamed the 'French Open' when players from outside France were allowed to play in it. The term 'Open' in a tournament generally implies the absence of restrictions.

The Tennis Grand Slam

Winning each of tennis's four most prestigious tournaments – the French Open, the US Open, Wimbledon and the Australian Open – in the same year is called a Grand Slam. Each of the four tournaments is actually referred to as a Grand Slam tournament. Very few players have been able to complete this feat.

A Basketball Gave Birth to Volleyball… Literally!

William G. Morgan is believed to have come up with the concept of volleyball in 1895. He wanted a sport that did not have the pushing and shoving that was becoming a part of basketball, which was already a rage in the US. While he worked out the rules of the sport, getting a ball for it was a problem. A basketball was used initially, but it was too heavy. It is believed that the bladder of a basketball was initially used for volleyball, until a ball was specifically developed for the sport. So yes, technically, basketball can claim to have given birth to volleyball. Incidentally, Morgan was a very close friend of James Naismith, the man who invented basketball.

The Golf Majors

Golf has four main tournaments, which are known as the 'Majors'. These are the Masters Tournament in April, the PGA Championship in May, the US Open Championships in June and the Open Championship in July. Interestingly, all four tournaments come in consecutive months from April to July.

The First Time Grand Slam Was Used for Any Sport

'Grand Slam' is a term that comes from the card game of bridge. However, it is now used to describe the feat of winning all major (generally four) tournaments in the same year across almost all sports. The term moved out of bridge and into mainstream sport when O.B. Keeler of the *Atlanta Journal* described Bobby Jones's feat of winning each of golf's four major tournaments in 1930 as a 'Grand Slam'. The term stuck.

The Largest Sports Stadiums in the World

The largest sports stadium in the world is the Narendra Modi Stadium, which has been designed for cricket and has a massive capacity of 1,32,000 people. Second to this is the Rungrado 1st of May Stadium in Pyongyang, DPR Korea (North Korea), which has a capacity of 1,12,000 and can host football as well as athletics.

When Olympic Medals Were Handed Out for Art

The Olympic Games are associated with sporting contests. However, for quite a while, Olympic medals were awarded for performances in the field of art. Between 1912–1948, there were Olympic medals awarded in different categories in the following fields:

Architecture
Literature
Music
Painting
Sculpturing

A Gold Medal for the Best Film? It Could Have Happened!

Olympic medals were awarded in various fields of art, and not just sports, in the Olympic Games between 1912–1948. And if Germany had its way, films would have been winning Olympic medals too. The German government under Adolf Hitler had proposed a film competition in the 1936 Olympic Games, but it was rejected. One wonders if it would have made the Oscars sweat!

Olympics in Melbourne, Equestrian Events in Stockholm!

Imagine an Olympics Games being hosted on a particular continent, with a single event being hosted in another part of the world? It happened in 1956. The Olympic Games were awarded to Melbourne, but a complication was that Australian quarantine laws required a six-month quarantine period for horses entering the country. That made it impractical to host the equestrian events at Melbourne, so it was decided to host the event in another country. The equestrian events for the 1956 Olympic Games were held in the same year, but in Stockholm. They were called the

Equestrian Games and even had a formal opening ceremony with the Olympic torch being brought in on horseback.

Basketball's Most Prestigious Tournament

Although basketball is played in many countries, it is more popular at the club level than at the national level, with international tournaments not attracting the sort of attention that club leagues and cups do. The National Basketball Association (NBA) of the US is considered to be the sport's most prestigious tournament. It comprises thirty teams and was founded in 1946.

The Only Canadian Team in the NBA

At the time of writing, twenty-nine of the thirty teams are from the US. The odd team out is the Toronto Raptors, which, as its name indicates, comes from Toronto.

No Nations in the Olympics? Well, It Sort of Happened

Until the 1908 Olympic Games, athletes participated in their individual capacity, rather than as representatives of a country. In some events like lawn tennis, players from different nations actually played together. This is why medal tallies of those Games are often confusing.

The Odd Case of Boxing in the 1904 Olympics

Boxing made its first appearance in the 1904 Olympic Games. But many statisticians do not include the boxing medals in the final medals tally. This is because of a number of irregularities in the competition, including allowing one boxer to participate in a weight category they did not belong to. Another boxer actually managed to compete in two different weight divisions, and another won medals under an assumed name. What's more, although participation was open to all nations, only US boxers competed.

Swimming in the 1896 Olympics Was Terrifying

In the 1896 Olympic Games, swimming was actually held in the open sea near the Bay of Zea. Conditions were not the greatest, and the water temperature dipped to a shocking 13 per cent. As per some reports, the water was so cold that one participant actually jumped out of the water, shouting, 'Jesus Christ, it is freezing.' Weather conditions were so bad that the rowing and yachting events had to be cancelled altogether.

Baseball's Most Major League!

Major League Baseball (MLB) is not only baseball's most prestigious tournament and league but also one of the US's biggest professional leagues. It comprises a total of thirty teams, fifteen in the National League (NL) and fifteen in the American League (AL). The champions of the NL and AL clash in a best of seven playoff in what is known as the World Series.

The Only Non-US team in Major League Baseball

Baseball's best known league, Major League Baseball (MLB), comprises a total of thirty teams. And just as in the NBA in basketball, twenty-nine of them are from the US and one is from Canada. The sole Canadian team in MLB is the Toronto Blue Jays.

The 'People's Olympics' of 1936

There were calls for a boycott of the 1936 Olympics in Berlin from a number of countries when Adolf Hitler came to power in

1933, to protest against his anti-Jew policies. Although this was not actually carried out, an alternate Olympics was planned, called the People's Olympics or the People's Olympiad, as a form of protest against the Olympics at Berlin. The games were to be hosted in Barcelona, Spain, and got the support of the USSR. However, the outbreak of the Spanish Civil War led to their cancellation.

When the Summer Olympics Were Hosted in the Winter!

Until 1956, all the Olympic Games had been hosted in the northern hemisphere. As these were also called the Summer Olympics, they were held in what was summer for that part of the world, between April and August. However, this was turned right on its head when the Australian city of Melbourne was awarded the Olympics in 1956. These were the first Olympics to be hosted in the southern hemisphere, where summer and winter occurred at rather different times. The summer games were therefore hosted from 22 November to 8 December, which was winter in many of the participating countries. No Summer Olympics have been contested later in the year.

The Only Olympics in an Odd-Numbered Year

Ever since their inception in 1956, the Olympics have been held at intervals of four years (unless cancelled) and in even-numbered years. The only time this has not happened was at Tokyo in 2021. The Tokyo Olympics were supposed to be held in 2020 but had to be postponed because of the COVID pandemic affecting most of the world.

The First Olympic Mascot... Woof!

Having a mascot is traditional for most sporting events these days. But this is a relatively modern trend. For a long time, sports events managed fine without any mascot. That changed in the 1972 Olympics with the introduction of the adorable dachshund, Waldi!

The Oldest Sport of Them All? Wrestle with This

There is no clear evidence of which sport is actually the oldest in human history, but many experts say that of all the sports that exist currently, wrestling in all probability is the oldest. Carvings and drawings depicting the sport that are almost 15000–20000 years old have been found in caves in Europe. Archery, running and swimming are also said to hark back thousands of years.

The Marathon of Archery Contests – Shoot Arrows for 24 Hours

Archery has a very special place in Japanese history. And some very special events too, including shooting at targets while on horseback (yabusame). But no archery contest (in perhaps any sport) can match the stamina and concentration levels demanded by oyakazu, where contestants try to hit the target as many times as possible – in a period of 24 hours. They literally shoot arrows all through the day and night. The record is believed to be 8,132 hits from a total of 13.053 arrows. That is almost 50 arrows being shot every hour.

Scoring in Archery: Hitting the Bullseye

The target in archery is generally circular and 1.2 metres in diameter. It is divided into ten concentric rings of different colours. In the centre of this is an area of 12.2 centimetres that is called the bullseye. Hitting the bullseye gets the highest score – 10 points. The number of points keeps decreasing with every circle – hitting the outermost circle gets only 1 point, and missing the target altogether gets no points at all. If an arrow hits the line dividing two circles, the archer gets the score of the higher circle. The archer with the highest score after a specific number of shots wins.

The Olympics Only One City Wanted to Host

There is generally a bitter contest between cities and nations to host the Olympics as the Games generate massive tourist attention and are also seen as a great way of showcasing a nation. However, such was the damage caused by the terrorist attack in the 1972 Olympics at Munich and so heavy was the financial burden on the 1976 Games on Montreal (it would take Canada decades to pay off the debts it took for the Games), that only one city bid for the 1984 Games – Los Angeles.

How the Olympics Went Corporate

Until the 1984 Games, the Olympics were always hosted with significant financial support from the government. However, following major financial mismanagement in the 1976 Olympics at Montreal, the 1984 Olympics were held without any financing from the government. A lot of the money for the Games came from corporate sponsors, and although some considered this to be a corruption of the Olympic spirit and did not like the idea of businesspeople having a major say in the event, this is the model that has been broadly followed ever since.

The Volcano that Cost a Nation its Olympic Ambitions

Mount Vesuvius is best known for having destroyed the ancient Roman city of Pompeii. But not many know that it also destroyed Italy's first ambition of hosting a modern Olympics. Rome had been awarded the 1908 Olympic Games, and preparations were in full swing when on 7 April 1906, Vesuvius erupted unexpectedly, destroying the city of Naples. The Italian government had to divert funds to provide aid to the city and as a result, had to admit that it did not have the resources to host the Olympics. The Games were moved to London!

The Olympics Return to Olympia After a Thousand Years... And Finally, a Woman Competes

The ancient Olympic Games were hosted in a stadium in Olympia. Women were not allowed to participate in them. But when the 2004 Olympic Games were awarded to Athens, it was decided to use the stadium (now renovated) in Olympia again. On 18 August 2004, an Olympic sport was held at the Olympia stadium after 1635 years. And in one of the most remarkable coincidences in sporting history, the first participant was a woman – Kristin Heaston of the United States in the women's shot put!

CHAPTER THREE

Great Champions

The First Sports Superstar?

Perhaps the first superstar of sport was Leonidas of Rhodes. The Greek attained legendary status by winning all three foot races in four consecutive Olympics from 164 BCE to 152 BCE. Leonidas participated in the Stade (about 200 metres), the Diaulos (twice the stade, so about 400 metres) and the hoplitodromos, a race of about 400 metres run in full armour (which added about 6 kilograms to the weight of the athlete). Such was Leonidas's domination of these three races that a historian of the period wrote that he made all theories of running seem obsolete. His collection of twelve victory wreaths is believed to be the biggest haul by any athlete in the ancient world. His command of the three races led to him being called 'Triastes' or the tripler!

The First-Ever Olympic Champion

There is some dispute about it, but the first recorded winner of an Olympic event is believed to be Coroebus of Elis, a baker and cook from Greece, who won a foot race called the stade in the first Olympics way back in 776 BCE. His reward was a wreath of olive leaves. He was honoured in his town of Elis, and after his demise, his grave had a very prominent place.

The First Woman Champion at the Olympics

Women were not allowed to participate in the ancient Olympic Games. However, the first female champion on record still belongs to the ancient Games – 396 BCE to be exact. This was Kynisca, the sister of the king of Sparta. Although she could not participate herself, she was allowed to enter a chariot in the chariot race event. Her team won the four-horse chariot race, so the victory was recorded in her name, although she herself did not participate in it.

The Athlete Who Sang, Danced and Won Everything at the Olympics!

The most successful Olympic athlete is an emperor. Roman emperor Nero (CE 37–68), who is actually better known for his eccentric lifestyle (he was accused of fiddling when Rome burnt), decided to participate in the Olympics in CE 67. Well, the Games were supposed to be held in CE 65 but Nero being an emperor, he bribed the Greek organizers to move them by two years to enable him to participate. And as he was emperor, he also introduced new events, which included singing and dancing. He also took part in chariot races, and although he was unable to finish, he was declared the winner on the rationale that he would have won HAD he finished. Oh, incidentally, he won all the events he participated in, and he participated in pretty much everything – some say he recorded more than a thousand victories! There are rumours that his competitors were told that they ran the risk of being executed if they defeated the emperor! Not surprisingly, his name was removed from the list of winners after his death, but he remains, so what if somewhat controversially, the most successful participant at a single Olympic Games.

Most Medals at the Olympics

Winning a single medal at the Olympic Games is a massive sporting achievement. Imagine winning several? Well, some athletes have won more than a dozen Olympic medals in their careers. The most successful Olympic athlete is US swimmer Michael Phelps, who has won a staggering 28 Olympic medals – 23 gold, 3 silver and 2 bronze. He did this across five Olympic Games from 2000 to 2016. Larissa Latynina of the erstwhile USSR has won the most Olympic medals by any woman. A gymnast, she won 18 medals (9 gold, 5 silver and 4 bronze) from 1956–64.

The Champ Who Kept an Eye on the Stopwatch and Not His Opponents

Paavo Nurmi of Finland was one of the greatest middle and long-distance runners of the 1920s. He was so far ahead of most of his competitors that after a stage, he actually started racing against himself instead of keeping an eye on his opponents. In those days, sports watches did not exist, and there were no large electronic scoreboards showing the time, so Nurmi actually ran with a stopwatch in the palm of his hand, checking his own speed at different intervals. It was a habit that annoyed his opponents immensely as it seemed to indicate that Nurmi was more concerned about his own timing rather than the presence of his competitors. But knowing him, 'the Flying Finn' (as he was called) was probably just that. It did seem to work – Nurmi is the only man to hold world records simultaneously in the mile, 5,000 metres and 10,000 metres, having achieved the feat in 1923. He also won a staggering nine gold and three silver medals in the Olympics from 1920–28.

The Man Who Invented the Modern Hurdling Technique

When you see hurdles races in athletics, it is common to see athletes clearing hurdles without breaking stride, with their leading leg going right over the hurdle. However, this was not always the case. In fact, in the late nineteenth century, most athletes stopped before the hurdle and hopped over it, jumping with both legs together. Credit for changing this to the modern style is given to the US's Alvin Kraenzlein, who used his leading leg to go over the hurdle. He used this technique effectively to win four individual gold medals at the 1900 Olympic Games.

The Greatest Rivalry in Sport?

The world of sport has seen some amazing rivalries, but by general consensus, nothing has quite matched the quality and longevity of the one between tennis players Martina Navralitova and Chris Evert, both of the US (although Navratilova was initially a Czech citizen). They first played each other at the Virginia Slims event at Akron in 1973 and played each other a total of 80 times in the next fifteen years, playing each other for the last time in the Virginia Slims event at Chicago in 1988. Such was their dominance of tennis that they were often the top two players in the world and no fewer than 60 of their 80 matches were played in the finals of tournaments. In the end, Navratilova finished 43–37 ahead in their rivalry. Quite remarkably, they were very good friends as well and even played as doubles partners.

The Most Successful Nations at the Olympic Games

In terms of winning medals, the US has been by far the most successful nation in the history of the Olympic Games, winning more than twice as many medals than any other nation and actually winning more medals than the second and third most successful nations. And this is despite missing the 1980 Olympic Games in Moscow, which it boycotted to protest against the then-USSR's invasion of Afghanistan. It does need to be kept in mind, though, that China and the USSR participated in very few Olympics.

Here are the ten most successful nations in Olympic history.

Rank	Nation	Olympics	Gold	Silver	Bronze	Total
1	United States	28	1,061	836	739	2,636
2	Soviet Union	10	440	357	325	1,122
3	Germany	25	285	326	363	974
4	Great Britain	29	285	315	315	915
5	China	11	262	199	173	634
6	France	29	226	258	280	764
7	Italy	28	217	188	213	618
8	Hungary	27	181	154	176	511
9	Russia	10	170	157	178	505
10	Japan	23	169	150	178	497

The First Modern Olympic Champion

While there is some uncertainty about who was the first person to win an Olympic event in the ancient Olympics, when it comes to the modern Olympics, we do know who was the first person to be declared a champion. The 1896 Olympic Games got underway on 6 April, and on that very day, they had their first official champion. James Connolly of the US became the first person in more than a thousand years to be called an Olympic champion when he won the triple jump.

When the Father of the Olympics Won Gold… Under Another Name

In the 1912 Olympic Games, medals were awarded for works of art too. And in the category of Mixed Literature, the gold medal was given to Germany's Georges Hohrod and Martin Eschbath for their work 'Ode to Sport'. However, what not too many know is that the authors were just a pseudonym adopted by the man considered by many to be the father of the Modern Olympic Games, Baron Pierre de Coubertin.

The Youngest Olympic Champion… And No One Knows His Name

He is the youngest person to win an Olympic gold medal, being a mere eight years old when he won. But no one knows his name. The Netherlands won the coxed pairs rowing event in the 1900 Olympics at Paris. They selected an eight-year-old boy (some say he was French) as their coxswain for the final. Although the Netherlands won, and the winning team was photographed, to this day, no one knows who the eight-year-old boy was. The age of the youngest Olympic champion in history is known. His name is not.

Legend Who Could Not Make His High School Team

There are many who consider Michael Jordan to be the greatest basketball player of all time. Well, he certainly was no child prodigy. He could not initially make his high school basketball team! Must have been some basketball team!!

The Most Versatile Athlete in Olympic History?

There have been athletes who have participated in different sports at the Olympic Games, but perhaps none has been as versatile as Carl Schuhmann of Germany at the 1896 Games. He participated in four different sports – athletics, weightlifting, gymnastics and racing. He began by competing in the long jump, triple jump and shot-put, but with limited success – his best was a fifth place in the triple jump (he finished last in the shot-put). A medal eluded him in what was called the two-handed weightlifting competition, where he finished joint fourth. But he really came into his own in gymnastics and wrestling. He won gold in the team gymnastic events of the horizontal bars and parallel bars and also won the individual gold in the vault. He then also won gold in the Greco-Roman wrestling event. Many called him the biggest star of the 1896 Olympics. It would be difficult for anyone to replicate his feat these days, given the level of specialization in sports.

The Only Player to Win a Grand Slam in Golf

Only one player has been able to win all four golf majors in the same year. This was Bobby Jones who won the Open Championship, the US Open and the US Amateur and the British Amateur championships, which were considered the major tournaments of the time, in 1930. Since then, no other player has been able to achieve this feat. The only player to come close to it was Tiger Woods, who won these four tournaments in a row but in different years – he won the US Open, the Open Championships and the PGA Championship in 2000 and then won the Masters in 2001. For a short while, he was the defending champion of all four tournaments, but he had not won them in the same year. Given the difficulty level of golf, many feel that the chances of a player winning the Grand Slam are paper thin!

Unbeaten for More than 500 matches – the Opponents Got 'Squashed'!

Long winning streaks are rare, especially in highly competitive sports. In tennis, the longest a player has gone without losing a match is 74 matches by Martina Navratilova in 1984. On the men's side, Bjorn Borg went unbeaten for 53 matches in 1977–78.

In men's football, Italy went 37 matches unbeaten from 2018 to 2021, although, remarkably, they could not qualify for the 2022 World Cup at Qatar. In cricket, the West Indies were unbeaten in 23 Test matches from 1982 to 1984. Boxing had Jimmy Wilde maintaining an unbeaten streak of 100 bouts from 1911 to 1915. But the most staggering winning streaks perhaps are squash legend Jahangir Khan and 400 m hurdles legend Edwin Moses. Jahangir Khan won a staggering 555 games between 1981 and 1985, which is considered to be the longest winning streak of matches by any professional athlete. But when it comes to the duration of staying unbeaten, hurdler Moses takes the lead. The bespectacled wonder was unbeaten from 1977 to 1987, winning 122 races. By some coincidence, his streak was a surprisingly symmetrical nine years, nine months and nine days.

Flagbearer at Three Olympics for Three Different Nations

The map of Europe underwent several changes following the collapse of the USSR and the eastern Bloc countries in the 1990s. And nothing represented this change better than Greco wrestling legend Aleksandr Karelin. He was the flagbearer for his country in the opening ceremony of three consecutive Olympics in 1988, 1992 and 1996. And each time, he carried a different flag for a different nation – he carried the USSR flag in 1988, the CIS flag in 1992 and the Russian flag in 1996. Interestingly, he won the gold medal in his event all three times. He was not the flagbearer in 2000 and finished with a silver. Coincidence?

Greatest Ice Hockey Player Ever, by Some Distance

When it comes to ice hockey, perhaps no one played it as successfully as Wayne Gretzky of Canada. He holds most of the scoring records in the National Hockey League (NHL), which is the sport's premier tournament. He has scored the most goals (894) and also the most goals in a single season (92), as well as the most assists (1,963) and the most assists in a season (163). In ice hockey, a player gets a point for scoring or providing an assist that led to a goal. Gretzky, not surprisingly, also has the highest points tally in NHL history with 2,857 (894 goals + 1,963 assists). But so far ahead is he of the competition that even if you removed all his goals, he would still have the most points in NHL history just based on his assists – his 1,963 assists give him 1,963 points, which are well ahead of Jaromir Jagr at second place with a total of 1,921 points (766 goals and 1,155 assists). No wonder they called him the Great Gretzky.

Going Out Unbeaten

Going out when you are still at the top is an art that few have been able to master. Most sportspeople tend to hang around for a bit too long, often suffering as a consequence. However, one athlete who timed his departure to perfection was boxing legend Rocky Marciano. The World Heavyweight Champion from 1952 to 1956, Marciano never lost a professional fight and ended with a record of 49–0. He remains the most high-profile sports personality to have retired unbeaten on a professional level.

11-1, 24-1…How India Hammered Teams in Hockey at the Olympics

While most sports are initially dominated by the team that invented the sport or where it is most popular, few teams have bossed a sport like India bossed field hockey at the Olympic Games from 1928 to 1956. The team did not just beat opponents, it thrashed them, running up an amazing record of six consecutive gold medals. India's dominance can be gauged by the way in which the team defeated opponents in Olympic finals: Netherlands were beaten 3-0 in 1928, a much-hyped German team was drubbed 8-1 in 1936, an equally highly rated Britain side was beaten 4-0 in 1948, and in 1952, Netherlands suffered a 6-1 hammering. Never was the Indian domination as marked as in the 1932 Olympic Games at Los Angeles. There were just three teams in the tournament – India, Japan and the host, the US, so every team was assured a medal anyway, and there was no final, just a league in which each team played the other once. That did not stop India from inflicting an amazing amount of carnage. The team beat Japan 11-1, and then hammered the US 24-1 in what was then the heaviest defeat ever recorded in international hockey.

From Hurdling to Bobsledding

Edwin Moses of the US is considered by many to be the greatest 400 metres hurdles runner in history, winning Olympic golds in 1976 and 1984, and winning 122 consecutive races between 1977 and 1987. Not too many know, however, that after retiring in 1988, Moses switched to winter sports and was so good at them that he won a bronze with the US bobsled team at the 1990 World Cup.

Cricket's OG Superstar Who Increased Ticket Rates

W.G. Grace was perhaps the first true superstar of cricket. A striking figure with his broad frame and long, flowing beard, he was literally synonymous with cricket in the late nineteenth and early twentieth century. Such was his fame and so popular was he that cricket grounds often came with the notice 'Admission: threepence. If WG Grace plays, admission: sixpence'. Imagine!

The Legendary Team That Dances before a Match

The beginning of a sporting encounter is a serious business. So serious that some teams have very elaborate build-ups to a match. These can range from simple huddles to singing songs, but perhaps the most famous pre-match routine belongs to the New Zealand Rugby Union team, popularly known as the All Blacks (they are always dressed in black). Before every match they play, the All Blacks line up in front of their opponents and perform a traditional Maori dance, called the Haka. It is an elaborate ritual and represents laying down a challenge to their opponents. Some consider the Haka to be aggressive and an attempt to intimidate, but most opponents face the New Zealand team and respect the ritual. Other teams from the region also have their versions of the Haka, but it is the All Blacks version that has cult status and is perhaps the most iconic opening ritual of any sport!

All Blacks performing the Haka

Football World Cup (FIFA World Cup) Champions

The first football World Cup (also known as the FIFA World Cup) was held in 1930 and has since grown to be one of the most important sporting events in the world. These are the nations that have won the tournament so far:

Year	Winners	Runners-up
1930	Uruguay	Argentina
1934	Italy	Czechoslovakia
1938	Italy	Hungary
1950	Uruguay	Brazil
1954	W. Germany	Hungary
1958	Brazil	Sweden
1962	Brazil	Czechoslovakia
1966	England	W. Germany
1970	Brazil	Italy
1974	W. Germany	The Netherlands
1978	Argentina	The Netherlands
1982	Italy	W. Germany
1986	Argentina	W. Germany
1990	W. Germany	Argentina
1994	Brazil	Italy
1998	France	Brazil
2002	Brazil	Germany
2006	Italy	France
2010	Spain	The Netherlands
2014	Germany	Argentina
2018	France	Croatia
2022	Argentina	France

The Man Who Changed the High Jump

Anyone who has seen the high jump will be familiar with how athletes run in towards the bar, then turn their back to it and push off the ground and attempt to leap backwards over the bar. It might be a very common sight now, but prior to 1968, no one had seen it. Most people simply ran straight to the bar and attempted to leap or 'roll' over it, often using a technique called the straddle. The man who changed it was Dick Fosbury, a US athlete who started using the backward leaping technique at college, much to the horror of his coaches. People made fun of him initially, with one writer saying that his method looked like an 'airborne seizure', and he also had to contend with rough landing surfaces as his technique involved landing on his back. However, he kept getting better, and when he won the gold medal at the 1968 Olympic Games with his new technique, which had been christened the Fobury Flop, he changed the world of high jumping forever. Today, almost every high jumper uses Fosbury's method, making him one of the most influential sportspersons of all time.

The Male Olympic Champ Who Became a Page 3 Sensation as a Woman

Caitlyn Jenner is a well-known celebrity and media personality today. However, before she 'came out' as transgender in 2015, Jenner was actually an Olympic champion. She was known as Bruce Jenner and won the men's decathlon event at the 1976 Olympic Games in Montreal, setting a world record in the process! Jenner would later disclose that she suffered from gender dysphoria from her youth and finally came out as a trans woman in 2015, saying, 'For all intents and purposes, I am a woman.'

The First Black World Champion

Although sport had seen a number of Black players, world champions by and large were white. This was because in a racially segregated world, most white athletes refused to compete against Black ones. Black athletes often ended up competing against other Black ones or against people of colour. This era of exclusion ended when Jack Johnson became the first Black to be declared a world champion in a high-profile and global sport – boxing. Johnson, who worked at the docks and exercised horses before turning to professional boxing, rose through the boxing ranks, and although many white boxers avoided him, he finally got his chance against World Heavyweight boxing champion Tommy Burns at Sydney in 1908. In front of a stunned, mainly white, crowd, Johnson beat Burns so badly that the police had to stop the bout in the 14th round. The world had its first major Black champion. That was not the end of it, though. Johnson's victory so outraged members of the white community that they made the unbeaten James Jeffries come out of retirement to fight Johnson and win the title back for the White Man. The two fought in 1910, in a fight labelled the Fight of the Century, and Johnson won easily, effectively burying the myth of White Superiority.

Sultan of the Sabre – the Greatest Swordsman of Them All

Fencing has seen some great champions, but perhaps the greatest of them all was Nedo Nadi of Italy. He is the only fencer to have won gold medals with each of the fencing swords (epee, sabre and foil) at the same Olympic Games. He won gold in the sabre at the age of eighteen (being the youngest to win the event) in the 1912 Olympics and then won what was then an unprecedented five gold medals at the 1920 Olympics at Antwerp – he won the individual foil and sabre and was part of the team that won the epee, foil and sabre events. It is believed that he did not enter the individual epee event because his father disapproved of the epee, calling it a crude and undisciplined weapon. His performance in the 1920 Olympics is, however, considered to be the greatest in fencing history and as close to perfection as humanly possible. He went professional after the Games, although he coached the Italian team with some success in the 1936 Olympics.

Cricket World Cup Winners

The cricket World Cup (also called the ICC World Cup) is one of the most prestigious tournaments in the sport. It has been won by the following countries so far:

Year	Winner	Runner-up
1975	West Indies	Australia
1979	West Indies	England
1983	India	West Indies
1987	Australia	England
1992	Pakistan	England
1996	Sri Lanka	Australia
1999	Australia	Pakistan
2003	Australia	India
2007	Australia	Sri Lanka
2011	India	Sri Lanka
2015	Australia	New Zealand
2019	England	New Zealand
2023	Australia	India

The Greatest Male Gymnast of Them All

In terms of achievements, no male gymnast can perhaps match Vitaly Scherbo of CIS and Belarus. He won six of the eight gymnastic golds available at the 1992 Olympics and remains the only gymnast to have won a world title in each of the eight gymnastic events for men between 1993 and 1995. A series of personal problems and injuries, however, meant that his career was over by 1997. Still in 1992–1995, he achieved more than any other male gymnast had.

From Sporting Superstars to Heads of State

While many sportspersons have tried their hands at politics, very few of them have had success in both fields on the scale that George Weah of Liberia and Imran Khan of Pakistan have. Weah is considered to be one of the greatest African football players of all time and is the only African player to have won the prestigious annual Ballon d'Or football prize given to the best football player in the world (he won in 1995). Weah also won accolades while playing for various well-known clubs such as Paris Saint-Germain and AC Milan. He moved to politics after retiring from football and won the presidential elections in 2018. He served as Liberia's president from 2028 to 2023, and is believed to be the only professional football player to have ever served as the head of a nation.

Pakistan's Imran Khan is considered to be his country's greatest ever cricket player and one of the greatest captains and all-rounders the sport has ever known. He led his country to notable wins over other teams and eventually to the cricket World Cup in 1992. He too joined politics after retiring from the sport, and although his initial foray was not successful, he became Prime Minister of Pakistan in 2018, a post he held until late 2022. He is the only international cricketer to have been elected head of state of his country.

A World Champion in Tennis on the Grass… and on the Table

He is best known as perhaps the greatest British tennis player of all time, but Fred Perry was adept at another kind of tennis too. He won Wimbledon three times in a row (1934–36) and was also the first tennis player to win each of the four Grand Slam tournaments (the French Open, Wimbledon, the US Open and the Australian Open). However, Perry was also a bit of a table tennis prodigy and was so good that he actually won the World Table Tennis championship in 1929 at the age of twenty. In fact, he was the only non-Hungarian to win the title in its first nine years. He focused on tennis without the table after that, and the rest, as they say, is history.

Winning Medals in Throws, Runs and Jumps… At the SAME Olympics

There are generally three types of events in athletics – runs (on the track), jumps (in the pit) and throws (in the field). And each type has its own specialist athletes. It is rare to see an athlete being proficient in all three. So imagine an athlete who not just competed in all three types of events at the Olympics but actually won medals in each. This was Mildred 'Babe' Didrikson in the 1932 Olympics. Perhaps the most versatile athlete of all time, she had qualified for all the events at the Olympics (100 metres, the 80 metres hurdles, high jump, javelin throw and discus throw) but was allowed to participate in only three. She chose the 80 metres hurdles (a run/sprint), the javelin throw (a throw) and the high jump (a jump). What's more, she won the 80 metres hurdles and the javelin and tied for first place in the high jump and lost the gold only on a technicality.

Wins a Gold in Hockey and Then Runs in the Athletics Relay

Richard John Carr, better known as Dickie Carr, was known for his speed. A good sprinter at school, he, however, focused on field hockey and was selected to play for the Indian hockey team in the 1932 Olympics at Los Angeles. He won the gold with the team, but such was his versatility that he also participated in athletics as part of the 4 x 100 metres relay team, although with less success – the relay team could not make it to the final.

The Champ Who Outscored the Scoreboard

Imagine doing so well that the scoreboard is not equipped to handle your performance? Well, that was what happened at the uneven bars event of gymnastics at the 1976 Olympic Games at Montreal. Scoring in gymnastic events was given by judges who awarded gymnasts scores out of 10 for their performance. When Romania's Nadia Comaneci finished a very impressive uneven bars routine in thirty seconds, the scoreboard showed 1.00. People were surprised and then realized that the judges had actually given her a perfect score – a 10 out of 10. However, as no one had ever scored a 10, the scoreboards at the stadium were equipped to show only three digits, two of which were after a decimal point. They could show every score from 0 to 9.99. Because a 10 was a perfect score, and no one could possibly score that, could they? Nadia showed that they could. Her performance changed gymnastic scoreboards all over the world, who now had to budget for perfection.

Winning Formula: Most Successful Formula One Drivers

A number of drivers have won the Formula One World Championships (the World Drivers' Championships) since the championships started in 1950. However, only a few have managed to win it multiple times. In fact, at the time of writing, only eleven drivers had won the title three or more times:

Driver	Titles	Years of Victory
Michael Schumacher (Germany)	7	1994, 1995, 2000, 2001, 2002, 2003, 2004
Lewis Hamilton (UK)	7	2008, 2014, 2015, 2017, 2018, 2019, 2020
Juan Manuel Fangio (Argentina)	5	1951, 1954, 1955, 1956, 1957
Alain Prost (France)	4	1985, 1986, 1989, 1993
Sebastian Vettel (Germany)	4	2010, 2011, 2012, 2013
Jack Brabham (Australia)	3	1959, 1960, 1966
Jackie Stewart (UK)	3	1969, 1971, 1973
Niki Lauda (Austria)	3	1975, 1977, 1984
Nelson Piquet (Brazil)	3	1981, 1983, 1987
Ayrton Senna (Brazil)	3	1988, 1990, 1991
Max Verstappen (The Netherlands)	3	2021, 2022, 2023

The 'Eternal World Record' That Is Unlikely to Be Ever Broken

Uwe Hohn of Germany (erstwhile East Germany) is said to hold the 'eternal world record' in athletics. That is because he set a javelin throw world record of 104.80 metres in 1984, becoming the first (and so far, only) athlete to throw the javelin beyond 100 metres. His achievement sent alarm bells ringing in the track and field authorities, who feared that longer throws could actually endanger athletes running on the track and even spectators in the stand. The design of the javelin was changed in 1986 to reduce the distance it could travel. Since then, not many have been able to get near Hohn's mark even though it is no longer considered an official world record. As his record is unlikely to be broken by any thrower, Hohn is said to hold athletics' 'Eternal World Record'.

The Mother and Daughter Who Competed against Each Other

Women competed in the Olympic Games for the first time in the 1900 Games at Paris. They had two individual events – golf and tennis. And the golf event witnessed a spectacle that has never been repeated – that of a mother and daughter competing against each other. The event was won by 22-year-old Margaret Abbott of the US, making her the first US woman to win an Olympic medal. In joint seventh place was the 43-year-old Mary Abbott, her mother. They remain the only mother and daughter to have competed against each other in the Olympics.

The Champ Who Did Not Know She Had Won in the Olympics

Margarat Abbott of the US was one of the first women to win an Olympic event, when she won the golf event at the 1900 Olympics, where women were allowed to compete for the first time. However, she was actually not aware that she was competing in the Olympic Games and had thought that it was just a routine tournament. She would not know that she was the first woman from the US to win an Olympic gold for the rest of her life. She passed away in 1955, unaware that she was an Olympic champion. Her children were informed of the fact much later by a researcher who discovered it.

The Champion Who Threw Away His Olympic Medal

Cassius Clay won the gold medal in the light heavyweight division in the 1960 Olympic Games at Rome. However, he dropped the gold medal into the Ohio River later in the year when he was refused service at a whites-only restaurant. He would go on to become one of the greatest athletes of all time and change his name to Muhammad Ali.

A Hockey Star on Ice and on Grass

Ferenc Szamosi of Hungary clearly had a special bond with hockey. He was part of the Hungarian ice hockey team that competed in the 1936 Winter Olympics. And when the Summer Olympics got underway, Szamosi was there again – this time as a part of the Hungarian field hockey team. Unfortunately, he won no medals.

The Greatest Cricketer of Them All?

In most sports, there emerge players who break previous records and set new ones. Cricket, however, has one figure whose record towers so far above everyone else's that most observers feel that it will never be even remotely matched. This is the record of Sir Donald Bradman of Australia. Considered by many to be the greatest cricketer of all time, Bradman had a batting average of 99.94 over 52 Test matches. In simple terms, this meant he scored an average of 99 runs every time he went out to bat. To get a measure of how far ahead this is of anyone else, consider the second highest batting average for a player with more than

50 Test matches is that of Herbert Sutcliffe, who averages 60.73 in 54 Test matches. In fact, in cricket, averaging more than 50 per innings in a Test match is supposed to be a sign of greatness. Bradman averaged almost twice as much.

The Youngest and Oldest Champion? They Are the Same Person (for a While, Anyway)

For a while, Ulrike Mayfarth of Germany held a very unique set of records. She became the youngest athlete ever to win the women's high jump in the Olympics (and also the youngest gold medal winner in an individual Olympics event) when she won the event in the 1972 Olympics at Munich at just sixteen years of age. Remarkably, she won the event again twelve years later in 1984 at Los Angeles, and at twenty-eight, became the oldest athlete to have won the women's high jump at the Olympics, although this record was later broken. Ronnie O'Sullivan of England did even better. When he won the prestigious UK Championships in 1993 at just seventeen years of age, he became the youngest person to have won the tournament. A long career was predicted for him, but not too many would have believed that thirty years later, O'Sullivan would win the tournament again, just short of his forty-eighth birthday, to become its oldest champion as well, while still being its youngest one. Incidentally, O'Sullivan is still playing so that 'oldest' record might change again!

Dominating Table Tennis by Using Only One Side of the Racket

In table tennis, players use both sides of the racket/paddle. However, for a long time, Chinese players dominated table tennis, playing with a grip that actually used only one side of the table tennis bat (or paddle). This was the 'penholder grip' in which the players wrapped the thumb and index number around the handle of the bat with the tips of both fingers coming together in a grip that was very similar to the one used by many of us to hold a pen. It is believed that the grip was endorsed by Chairman Mao Zedong himself, who had given his approval to a coaching manual that recommended it. The grip meant that the players could use only one side of the bat and literally had no backhand, but until the mid-eighties, the world had no answer to it. It was only after Sweden beat China in the 1989 World Championships that the Chinese moved to a more conventional grip with the palm wrapped around the handle of the bat (also called the 'Western' or the 'Shakehand' grip).

The Running Tribe

The Kalenjin tribe of Kenya and Uganda is nicknamed the Running Tribe by many writers. This is because of the number of running champions that have come from the Kalenjin. In fact, most of Kenya's legendary long-distance runners have come from this tribe. As per some estimates, almost 40 per cent of the medals won at major events from 1980 onwards in distances of 800 metres and above have been won by members of the Kalenjin tribe. No one is really sure of what makes this tribe special as there are other tribes in the same area and conditions, but whenever a Kalenjin appears at a long distance race, other competitors turn wary.

The One Cricketer Who Was Almost as Good as Three!

Test cricket is played over five days with each team getting a chance to bat. Each team has eleven players, each of whom normally gets a chance to bat, and the total score of the team is the sum of the scores of each player along with any penalties on the other team. Now, imagine a player so dominant that he scored almost one-fourth of the total score of his team! That was Sir Donald Bradman of Australia. Holder of the highest batting average in Test cricket (99.94), Bradman, scored 24.28 per cent of his team's runs during his career. No one else with as long a Test career has even managed 19 or 20 per cent. In essence, if you dismissed Bradman, you had got one-fourth of his team out. One-fourth of eleven players is 2.75. That was what one Bradman was equal to – almost three batsmen!

The Twins Who Dominated Canoeing

Few siblings have dominated a sport like Peter and Pavol Hochschroner of Slovakia. The twins are considered to be the greatest canoeing pair in history. They won the Olympic gold medal in the C2 event in 2000, 2004, 2008 and 2012 and finished third in 2012. They also won the World Cup title ten times, which is a record.

One Athlete Who Qualified for All Track and Field Events

The 1932 Olympics had five individual track and field events for women – the 100 metres, the 80 metres hurdles, high jump, javelin throw and discus throw. Amazingly, one athlete, Mildred 'Babe' Didrikson of the US qualified for all five events. The rules allowed her to participate in only three, but her achievement remains unprecedented.

Tennis Players Who Have Completed a Grand Slam

Only five players have ever completed the feat of winning tennis's four major titles (the French Open, the US Open, Wimbledon and the Australian Open) in the same year. More have been able to win the titles in a row across two years, but only five have been able to achieve the classic singles Grand Slam, which involves winning all four titles in the same year. These are:

- Don Budge (1938)
- Maureen Connolly (1953)
- Rod Laver (1962 and 1969)
- Margaret Court (1970)
- Steffi Graf (1988)

Rod Laver's feat of winning the Grand Slam twice remains unmatched, and many say it is unlikely to be replicated.

The Greatest Tennis Champions

Success in tennis is measured by the number of Grand Slam (French Open, US Open, Wimbledon and Australian Open) tournaments a player wins. In men, this record is held by Novak Djokovic of Serbia, who has won 23 tournaments at the time of writing. He is followed by Rafael Nadal of Spain with 22 tournaments. In women, the record is held by Margaret Court with 24 Grand Slam titles, with Serena Williams in second place with 23 titles.

The Men's Tennis Player Who Won the Most Matches and Tournaments

Speak to people of the greatest men's tennis player of all time, and it is a fair chance that most will talk of the likes of Rod Laver, Bjorn Borg, Roger Federer, Rafael Nadal and so on. However, in terms of victories, no men's player has won more matches and tournaments than Jimmy Connors of the US. In a career spanning more than two decades (1972–1993), Connors won a staggering 1,274 matches and 109 tournaments – more than any male player in the Open era.

The Greatest Golf Champion?

The measure of the greatness of a golf player is the number of 'Major' tournaments (the Masters, PGA Championship, US Open and the Open Championship) that the player has won. By that measure, Jack Nicklaus of the US is the greatest golf player of all time, having won no fewer than 18 Majors. Tiger Woods comes second with 15 and Walter Hagen third with 11.

Being the Boss in Singles, Doubles and Mixed Doubles – the Boxed Set Champs!

While the singles champions get the most attention in tennis (and in other sports), there are some players who excel not just in singles but also in doubles (where two players play against two others) and mixed doubles (where a pair of players from each gender play a similar pair). The ability to win all three titles – singles, doubles and mixed doubles – at every Grand Slam tournament (US Open, French Open, Wimbledon and Australian Open) is referred to as a 'Boxed Set'. It is so rare that only three players in tennis history have been able to achieve it, and no male tennis player ever has. These three are Margaret Court, Doris Hart and Martina Navratilova.

Beating Dad to Grab a Gold Medal

The 1912 Olympic Games witnessed a rare occurrence in the individual single shot event. The event was won by Alfred Swahn of Sweden. One of the people he defeated to win the event was Oscar Swahn, his 64-year-old father, who finished fourth. Oscar Swahn would go on to become the oldest person to win a medal in Olympic history when he won a silver medal in the 1920 Olympic Games at the age of seventy-two.

The Most Valuable Player (MVP) of the NBA... Unanimously

One of the most prestigious individual honours in the NBA is for the title of the most valuable player (MVP) of the season. A player is chosen based on votes from select sportswriters and mediapersons. Needless to say, there is a great deal of debate and disagreement over the selection. The 2015–16 season, however, saw a massive surprise when Stephen Curry of the Golden State Warriors was named the MVP unanimously. All 131 people who voted had Curry at first place.

Five World Records in 45 Minutes – 'The Greatest 45 Minutes in Sport'

There have been some amazing achievements in the history of sport, but very few can match what Jessie Owens delivered on 25 May 1935. On that day, Owen broke five world records and equalled another. Actually, he did it in a mere 45 minutes. Owen was participating in the Big Ten Championships,. He ran the 100 yard dash at 3.15 pm, and equalled the world record of 9.4 seconds.Ten minutes later, at 3.25 pm, he set a world record of 8.13 metres in the long jump. Another nine minutes later, at 3.34 pm, he ran the 220 yard dash at 20.3 seconds, another world record. And as this was actually faster than the 200-metre world record (which was a shorter distance than 220 yards), he was awarded the world record for the 200 metres too. At 4 pm, 45 minutes after he had started his record-setting spree, Owens won the 220 yard hurdles in a world record time of 22.6 seconds. Again, this was below the 200 metres hurdles record, so he was credited with breaking that one as well. So in a period of 45 minutes from 3.15 pm to 4.00 pm, the 21-year-old Owen had set five world records and equalled another. He also had become the first man to jump beyond 8 metres and run the 220 yard hurdles in under 23 seconds. All this when he had a slight problem with his back. Owens won four gold medals at the Berlin Olympics in 1936, but his performance in the Big Ten Championships that day is still hailed as the greatest 45 minutes in sport!

Most Medal-Led Athlete at a Single Olympic Games

The most medals won by an athlete at an Olympic Games is eight. And rather remarkably, this figure has been achieved twice by the same athlete, in successive Olympic Games. Michael Phelps of the United States won six gold and two silver medals in swimming at the 2004 Olympic Games and then won eight gold medals in swimming in the 2008 Games. In terms of total medals won at a single Games, only one other athlete has matched this – Alexander Dityatin in men's gymnastics in the 1980 Olympics, where he won three golds, four silvers and a bronze.

Michael Phelps

Be It Summer or Winter, He Wins at the Olympics

Eddie Eagan might not exactly be a household name when it comes to sport, but he holds a record that is unlikely to be matched. Eagan is the only athlete to have won a gold medal at the Olympic Games (also called the Summer Olympics) as well as the Winter Olympics in different events. He won the light heavyweight boxing gold medal in the 1920 Olympics. Twelve years later, he was part of the four-man US team that won the gold in the 1932 Olympics. The only other athlete to have won gold medals in both the Winter and Summer Olympics is Gillis Grafstrom of Sweden, but he won in men's figure skating, which was part of the Summer Olympics in the 1920 Games and was moved to the Winter Olympics when they began in 1924.

The Only Player to Score a Century in NBA Basketball

Only one player has ever scored 100 points in a NBA basketball match. That honour goes to Wilt Chamberlain, who, in 1962, scored exactly 100 points for the Philadelphia Warriors against the New York Knicks. The extent of Chamberlain's achievement can be understood by the fact that no other player has ever scored even 85 points – Kobe Bryant is second with 81 points for the Los Angeles Lakers against the Toronto Raptors in 2006.

Three Generations of Olympic Hockey Stars

When Erwin Keller won a silver medal with the German team in field hockey at the 1936 Olympics, he perhaps did not know that he was the first of three generations of players from his family to end up on the hockey medal podium at the Olympics. His son, Carsten Keller, won the gold with West Germany in the same event in 1972, and his grandson, Andreas Keller, also won the hockey gold with Germany in 1992! That's one family with an eye for the hockey goal.

Winning at the Summer and Winter Olympics

There have been a number of athletes who have participated in the Winter as well as Summer Olympics. And a few have been able to succeed and win medals at both. But only one person has won medals at both Olympics and in the same year at that. This was Christa Luding-Rothenburger of East Germany, who won gold and silver in speed skating at the Calgary Olympics in 1988 and then picked up a silver in the Summer Olympics at Seoul in the women's cycling match sprint event. She remains the only athlete to have won medals at both the Winter and Summer Olympics in the same year.

The Most Dominant Gold Medalist Ever?

Natalya Lisovskaya's victory in the women's shot-put event was perhaps the most empathic in any event in athletics history. She won the gold, but all her six efforts were better than the best of all her opponents. Any of her puts could have won her the gold!

No Shoes? No Problem! Will Still Win a Marathon Gold

Abebe Bikila of Ethiopia had a tricky problem before the marathon event of the 1960 Olympics. The shoes he had purchased for the race were very uncomfortable and gave him blisters. His solution was simple – he ran the 42,195 metres race barefoot. Not only that, he won the race and set a world record of 2 hours, 15 minutes and 6.2 seconds. And he wasn't in the least bit tired either. Much to the surprise of the crowd, who were used to seeing athletes collapse in exhaustion at the end of the long race, Bikila actually did some stretching exercises and ran on the spot, looking as fresh as a daisy. He later said that he could have run another 10–15 kilometres. Four years later, Bikila was running in the marathon again, and this time, he had shoes that were comfortable. The result was another gold medal and another world record. He will always be known as the barefoot runner, though.

Most Points in the NBA

LeBron James has scored the most points in the NBA. At the time of writing, he had scored 38,652 while playing for Cleveland Cavaliers, Miami Heat and Los Angeles Lakers. He and Kareem Abdul-Jabbar are the only two players to have totalled more than 38,000 points in the NBA.

The Greatest Wrestler of Them All?

Sports has its share of legends, and one of them is Aleksandr Karelin of Russia. In terms of a single person dominating a sport throughout their career, there cannot have been too many better than the massive Karelin. He competed in the super heavyweight category of Greco-Roman wrestling, and at the senior level, his record was an astonishing 887 wins and just two defeats (both by just a single point). He won three consecutive gold medals at the Olympics in 1988, 1992 and 1996 and might have won even a fourth in 2000 but for a controversial loss in the final. In the World Championships, he was never beaten and won 9 titles. He was also undefeated for thirteen years prior to his defeat in the 2000 Olympics and such was his dominance that in six of those years, no opponent had even been able to score a point against him.

Most Valuable Player (MVP) Most Times

Kareem Abdul-Jabbar is the only player to have been voted most valuable player (MVP) of the NBA six times. Bill Russel and Michael Jordan have been named MVP five times each, while Wilt Chamberlain and LeBron James have got the title four times apiece.

The Tallest Player in a Sport for Tall People

Basketball is known as a sport for tall people, with most players being well above six feet tall (the average height of an NBA player is six and a half feet). The tallest of them all, however, was Georghje Muresan, who stood a towering 7 feet 7 inches and played in the NBA from 1993 to 2000. Muresan's remarkable height is attributed to a pituitary gland disorder.

Did I Actually Win an Olympic Medal?

The 1900 Olympic Games were riddled with confusion. Hosted in Paris, the events in the Games were spread over a massive five months (recent Olympics generally span a fortnight), and the Olympic status of many events was not highlighted. As a result, many winners did not even know that they were Olympic champions, although they were shown as such in the records.

Stepping Aside for His Brother

Britain's Doherty brothers, Laurence and Reginald, dominated men's tennis in the late nineteenth and early twentieth centuries. However, when they were drawn to play against each other in the semi-finals of the 1900 Olympic Games at Paris, Reginald stepped aside to let his younger brother, Laurence, go into the final (which he later won). The brothers, however, joined forces to win the doubles competition.

Tennis's First Family

Well before Venus and Serena Williams dominated women's tennis, Laurel and Reginald Doherty of Britain called the shots in men's tennis in the late nineteenth and early twentieth centuries. The brothers won nine of the ten Wimbledon men's titles contested between 1897 and 1906, with Reginald winning four times in a row from 1897–1900, and Laurence five times in a row from 1902–1906. They also won the doubles title eight times between 1897–1905. The brothers also won the Olympics doubles in 1900, with Laurence winning the singles after Reginald withdrew in the semi-final against him!

The First Women in the Modern Olympics

The Olympics were mainly for men, and there were no women allowed in the first modern Olympic Games in 1896. Women were allowed in the 1900 games at Paris. The first women to compete are believed to be Filleaul Brohy and Marie Ohnier in croquet, where women competed alongside men.

The Five Foot Three Inch NBA Wonder

Basketball is seen as a sport for tall people, and the average height of a basketball player is six feet six inches. So imagine a basketball star who is a mere five feet and three inches in height? That was Muggsy Bogues, who played in the NBA from 1987 to 2001. He was very good too, finishing in the top seven assists list for six consecutive seasons. It can be done!

A Grand Slam? She Won a 'Golden' Grand Slam

Steffi Graf of Germany was the last single's tennis player to achieve the feat of a Grand Slam – winning tennis's four major tournaments in the same year. She did so in 1988. What makes her achievement extra special, however, is that she also won the gold medal in the Olympics tennis event that year. Many refer to her achievement as the Golden Grand Slam. It is extremely unlikely to be replicated as the Olympics take place only once every four years.

The Boxing Champion Who Captained England in Cricket

J.W.H.T. Douglas of England has a unique place in sport. Although there are many who have succeeded in different sports, few have achieved the level of success Douglas did and that too in sports as radically different as boxing and cricket. Douglas excelled at both sports and at the same time. He made his debut for Essex county in 1901, and within a few years, was being seen as an England prospect, as a determined batsman and a very good bowler. He continued making remarkable progress in boxing too, and in 1908, representing Britain in the Olympics, he won the middleweight gold medal. He went on to not only play cricket for England but even captain the team with some success. He was a rather defensive batsman, though, which led to many nicknaming him 'Johnny Won't Hit Today', a name which clashed with his boxing achievements, where he hit frequently. And hard.

The Only Cricketer to Score 400 in a Test Match and 500 in a First-Class Match

Brian Lara of the West Indies holds a unique record in cricket. He is the only batter to have scored 400 in a Test match (against England in 2004) and 500 in a first-class match (for Warwickshire against Durham in 1994). Quite remarkably, no other batter has achieved this feat.

Most All England Badminton Titles

The All England Badminton Championships is the most prestigious badminton tournament in the world. And in the men's section, no one has won it more often than Indonesia's Rudy Hartono, who won it a record eight times between 1968–1976. Erland Kops of Denmark won the men's singles seven times between 1958–67. Among the modern players, Lin Dan of China won the title six times between 2004 and 2016. In the women's singles, Meriel Lucas of England won the ladies' singles a staggering ten times from 1899–1910, with Judy Devlin (who represented the US and then England) winning it seven times between 1954–1966.

The Most Successful Baseball Team

The most successful team in baseball history is the New York Yankees, which won baseball's biggest tournament, World Series, a total of 27 times. The St. Louis Cardinals are second with 11 wins.

The Most Home Runs in Baseball

The home run is one of the most dramatic moments of a baseball match. It occurs when either the batter hits the ball out of the ground (a bit like hitting a six in cricket) or circles all bases and reaching the home plate without a fielding error. Barry Bonds holds the record for the most home runs hit in Major League Baseball (MLB), baseball's most prestigious league. He struck a total of 762 home runs. Hank Aaron comes second with 755 and Babe Ruth third at 714.

The Most Versatile Athlete of All Time

She won the Wimbledon ladies' single titles five times (the first when she was only fifteen in 1887), played twice for England's women's hockey team in 1899 and 1900 (scoring two goals in a win over Ireland), won the British Ladies Amateur Golf Championship in 1904 and won the silver medal in the women's double archery in the 1908 Olympics. Still want to know why many consider Charlotte 'Lottie' Dod to be one of the most versatile athletes of all time?

Breaking the World Record a World Record 35 Times

Sergey Bubka of the erstwhile USSR is one of the greatest athletes of all time. He excelled in the pole vault, where he stunned the world by setting a total of 35 indoor and outdoor world records between 1984 and 1994. No athlete has set so many world records in a single event. There is a rumour that Bubka always increased his previous world record by a centimeter to get a special bonus from the USSR government. Whether true or not, it resulted in him taking the world record from 5.85 metres to 6.15 metres! Imagine someone breaking a world record (generally their own) once every few months? That was Sergey Bubka from 1984–94.

Father and Son Win Gold and Silver

The Star Class yachting event of the 1948 Olympics was literally a father and son thing. The gold medal was won by Hilary Smart and his son, Paul Smart, of the US while the silver went to Cuba's Carlos de Cardenas and his son, Carlos de Cardenas.

Little Lovely Inge… The Youngest Ever to Win an Olympic Medal on Her Own

There have been some very young Olympic medallists, generally as part of a team of much older participants (an eight-year-old boy won a rowing gold with the Netherlands team in 1900), but when it comes to winning an Olympic medal in an individual event, the record is held by the one famous as 'Lille Henrivende Inge' (or 'Little Lovely Inge'). This is Inge Sorensen, who at the age of twelve, won a bronze medal in the 200 metres breaststroke in the 1936 Olympics in Berlin.

The Ultimate Long-Distance Runner?

The three longest running races in athletics are the 5,000 metres, the 10,000 metres and the marathon (42,195 metres). Winning all three at the same event is rare. In fact, only one athlete has ever won all three at the same Olympics. That was Emile Zatopek of Czechoslovakia in the 1952 Olympics.

Running the Marathon for the First Time Ever… And Winning an Olympic Gold

Although he was legendary as a 5,000 metres and 10,000 metres champion, Emile Zatopek of Czechoslvakia had never run in a marathon. However, when he won the 5,000 metres and 10,000 metres at the 1952 Olympics at Helsinki, Zatopek decided to 'try' the marathon. At a little more than 42 kilometres, the marathon was a significantly longer race – almost three times the distance of 5,000 metres and 10,000 metres put together. Still, Zatopek went ahead and entered the event. He did not know much about it so noted down the number of Jim Peters of Britain, who was considered the best marathon runner in the world. During the race, Zatopek is believed to have caught up with Peters and asked if his speed was good. A surprised Peters said it wasn't fast enough. Zatopek thought about this and calmly ran past Peters and went ahead and won the gold by some distance. Peters, interestingly, could not finish the race. Zatopek's triple title swoop of the 5,000 metres, 10,000 metres and the marathon remains unmatched to this day, but his victory in the marathon remains even more remarkable. He had never run the distance. He had simply turned up, run and beaten the best!

The Gymnastics Legend Who Refuses to Retire

Because of the nature of the sport, which requires both flexibility and strength, it is rare to see gymnasts staying in the sport beyond the age of twenty-eight. In fact, most gymnasts generally call it quits by twenty-five. Which is why Oksana Chusovitina of Uzbekistan is an utter aberration. Easily the greatest gymnast of all time in terms of sheer longevity at the highest level, Chusovitina is the only gymnast to ever compete in eight Olympic Games. She

Oksana Chusovitina

entered the 1992 Olympics at a time when most of the leading gymnasts today had not even been born. She has also competed in 16 World Championships and is one of the few gymnasts to have returned to the sport after giving birth to a child. At the time of writing, she is planning to appear in the 2024 Olympics as well. She will be forty-nine!

The 'Dream Team' That Became Real

The term 'dream team' is often used to describe fantasy teams that comprise players from different teams and eras, but the term gained popularity when it was used for the US basketball team in the 1992 Olympic Games. This was the first time professional basketball players were allowed in the Olympic Games, and as a result, the US basketball team came with the likes of Michael Jordan, Magic Johnson, Larry Bird and Charles Barkley. The team was so packed with legends that the term 'dream team' was used to describe it and has since gained immense popularity! Incidentally, the team went on to win the gold easily, averaging 117 points per match and never calling a timeout.

The High Jump Legend Who Hated Attention… and Hollywood

One of the most popular winners at the 1928 Olympic Games was Ethel Catherwood of Canada, who won the women's high jump event. The very good-looking Ethel was dubbed 'The Saskatoon Lily' because she liked to wear a pure white uniform. Although her victory triggered off a wave of celebrations in her hometown, Catherwood tended to avoid publicity, and when asked about the prospects of her joining Hollywood, is believed to have replied: 'I would rather gulp poison.' She did not like giving interviews and did not even attend the ceremony in which she was inducted into the Canadian Hall of Fame. She moved to the US, and so reclusive was she that her own hometown knew of her demise almost seven months after she had passed away in 1987.

Breaking the World Record by Such a Margin that Even the Measuring Equipment Failed!

'Records are made to be broken' is a cliché that is often repeated by sports writers and commentators. But sometimes a record is broken so thoroughly that even the person who has broken it cannot quite fathom what they have done and how. This is exactly what happened in the men's long jump event in the 1968 Olympic Games at Mexico. The favourites for the event were Igor Ter-Ovanesyan of the erstwhile USSR and Ralph Boston of the US, both of whom also held the joint world record of 27 feet, 4 ¾ inches (8.35 meters). No one in the world had jumped even close to 28 feet (about 8.53 meters), or even past 27 feet (8.23 meters) in the Olympics - Boston held the Olympic record at 26 feet, 7 ¾ inches (8.12 meters). Although the 1968 Games were held in Mexico City at high altitude, which is believed to assist events that involve sprinting (including the long jump), people were not expecting the world record in the event to be broken by too dramatic a margin. Bob Beamon of the US, however, had other ideas. On a clouded day with occasional rains, the long jumper began his run to the long jump pit muttering 'don't foul, don't foul' (the three jumpers before him had all fouled) and then tore down the stretch at a frightening speed. He then took off, soaring to a height of almost six feet as per some spectators, and as people watched in astonishment, hit the hit with such force that he actually bounced out of it. 'It can't be', muttered shocked officials. So far had Beamon leapt that the special optical measuring device used for the event was not able to calculate the distance, and an old fashioned tape measure had to be brought out.

The result was then displayed on the scoreboard – 29 feet 2 ½ inches (8.90 meters), almost 2 feet more than the world record, and almost 2.5 feet past the former Olympic record. As the crowd gasped in amazement, stunned former world record holder Igor Ter-Ovanesyan told Britain's Lynn Davies 'Compared to this jump, we are as children'. Davies, for his part, said to Beamon: 'You have destroyed this event.'

Beamon himself was not aware of what he had done as he did not understand the metric system, and felt that while his jump was good, others would match it. When he truly understood what he had done, he collapsed in shock on the track. He had jumped more than 29 feet when no one had even been able to jump 28 feet. His world record would stay for almost 23 years, finally broken by Mike Powell of the US in 1991 at the World Championship. To this day – more than fifty years later – no one has jumped further at an Olympic Games!

CHAPTER FOUR

Such Good Sports

When All Teams March as One

In the Olympic Games, while the athletes of nations walk under their nations' flags in the opening ceremony, they enter the stadium together in no particular order in the closing ceremony. Credit for this idea is given to John Ian Wing, an apprentice carpenter in Australia. It was first used in the 1956 Games in Melbourne.

The Athlete Who Lost a Medal and Then Searched for the Winner

The 110 metres hurdles at the 1932 Olympics saw the new photo-finish technology being used to decide the medal winners. And this resulted in the results being changed. Jack Keller of the US, who had been originally given the bronze medal in the race, was found to have actually finished behind Donald Finley of Great Britain, who was initially believed to have finished fourth. Keller actually went out looking for Finley in the Olympic village and gave him his medal!

Father Takes Time Out for Son, Son Wins Gold!

Bill Havens had been chosen for the United States in the coxed eights rowing event in the 1924 Olympic Games. However, he decided to stay back because he and his wife were expecting their first child. The US team went on to win the gold medal. Twenty-eight years later, a US athlete won the gold medal in the

C-1 10,000 metres canoeing competition in the 1952 Olympic Games. It was Frank Havens, the child for whom Bill Havens had missed the 1924 Olympics.

The Champ with a Heart of Gold

The rowing event of the 1928 Olympics at Antwerp saw an amazing display of sporting spirit. In the quarterfinals of the single sculls, Australia's Henry Pearce, who was one of the favourites for the gold, was well ahead when he heard shouts from the crowd. He looked and saw a row of ducks in the water ahead of him. This was a race, and his qualification for the final depended on the result, but Pearce still slowed down and leaned on his oars, letting the ducks cross his path unharmed and then resumed rowing. His competitors took advantage of his break and went ahead of him, but such was Pearce's prowess that he overtook them again and finished first. He went on to win the gold medal.

Giving up a Gold Medal for Fair Play

Britain's Judy Guiness had won the gold medal in the women's individual foil in fencing in the 1932 Olympics. However, in an astonishing show of fair play, Guinness then went and told the officials that they had failed to count two hits made by her opponent, Ellen Preis of Austria. The two hits cost Guiness the gold medal and relegated her to silver.

Getting a Lift on the Track from Your Formula One Rival!

Ayrton Senna of Brazil and Nigel Mansell of Britain were bitter rivals in Formula One, often facing off against each other in a number of races. However, when Senna's car broke down at the

British Grand Prix at Silverstone, Mansell, who had won the race, actually gave his rival a lift in his own car, taking him to the pits. It remains one of the most famous lifts given in Formula One history.

When Dad Helped Him Finish the Race

One of the most emotional moments in the history of sport had absolutely nothing to do with the result of a race. Britain's Derek Redmond had arrived in the 1992 Olympics at Barcelona as one of the favourites for the 400 metres. However, in the semi-finals of the event, his hamstring snapped. Although barely able to run, he refused to get off the track and tried to hop to the finish. As an amazed stadium watched, a man ran in from the crowd and lent Redmond his shoulder, supporting him and gently walking him to the finish line. It was his father, Jim.

The Gold Medallist Who Shared His Place on the Podium with a Bronze Medallist

The light heavyweight boxing competition in the 1984 Olympics witnessed an amazing moment of sportsmanship during the medal presentation ceremony. The winner of the gold medal, Anton Josipovic of Yugoslavia, actually pulled bronze medal winner Evander Holyfield of the US to stand alongside him at the top of the podium. Holyfield had been controversially disqualified in the semi-finals and was considered by many to have been the best boxer in the event. He would go on to be a legendary boxing champion in the 1990s.

When the Gold Medallist Carried the Silver Medallist to the Podium

The dressage event in the 1952 Olympics was notable for being open to all participants, and not just army officers. It also featured one of the rare occasions when women competed directly against men.

The silver medal was won remarkably by Lis Hartel of Denmark who had suffered from a polio attack and was paralysed beneath her knees. She had to be helped into and off her saddle right through the event. Her disability did not stop her from becoming one of the leading riders in the world and also earned her the admiration of her opponents. When the winners rode up to receive their medals at the 1952 Olympics, gold medal winner Henry Saint Cyr dismounted and helping Hartel off her horse and carried her to the podium. As the spectators applauded, Hartel broke down and wept, providing the Olympics with one of its most memorable moments.

He Kept Defeating the Chinese... And They Loved Him

Jan Ove Waldner of Sweden was instrumental in ending the Chinese domination of table tennis in the late eighties and early nineties. Famous for his great technique, Waldner was known for beating Chinese players and won the World Championships, as well as the Olympics. Despite this, he was incredibly well-loved in China, and was affectionately called Lao Wan (the Evergreen Tree) and also owns a restaurant in China called the W Bar.

The Teams That Refused to Salute Hitler at the 1936 Olympic Games

The 1936 Olympic Games at Berlin are widely believed to have been staged to showcase Hitler's regime. The German leader was often in the stadium and personally congratulated many athletes. He was very much present at the march past of the teams when the Games were inaugurated. In front of a massive crowd, all the teams that marched past Adolf Hitler raised their arms in the Nazi salute to greet him. Only two contingents are believed to have not done so – the US and India.

The Man Who Refused to Attack an Opponent's Injury

On the eve of the final of the men's open class category of judo, Mohamed Ali Rashwan of Egypt learnt that his opponent in the final, the legendary Yasuhiro Yamashita of Japan had torn a right calf muscle. When the pair clashed in the final, many expected Rashwan to attack the injury of the Japanese. He, however, steadfastly refused to do so, considering it unfair. He lost the bout and ended with a silver medal, but his gesture was widely praised. He was awarded an International Fair Play Committee award, a United Nations fair play award and was included in the International Judo Federation Hall of Fame. In 2019, the Japanese ambassador presented him with the prestigious Order of the Rising Sun. To this day, Rashwan says he has no regrets about his decision, although it probably cost him a gold medal.

A Great American Basketball Team That Never Played in the NBA

The Harlem Globetrotters are considered a legendary basketball team in the US. Formed in the late 1920s, they were closely associated with the African American community and have played thousands of matches. Quite remarkably, however, this team has never played in the NBA and is known mainly for playing exhibition matches, with a playing style marked by comedy and amazing displays of skill. They are perhaps the world's most famous exhibition sports team and have played more than 20,000 exhibition matches all over the globe. They are more about showcasing skill and entertainment than about competing. Come to think of it, that's what most sports are really about.

Harlem Globetrotters with the then US president George H.W. Bush and Arnold Schwarzenegger, 1992

The Best Rain Break Ever

Having play stopped by rain is an experience no spectator or sports fan likes. However, some might not have minded when the skies darkened and rain fell on the Centre Court at Wimbledon in 1996 during a quarter final match between Richard Krajcek and Pete Sampras. As spectators waited patiently for play to resume, they were surprised to see legendary pop star Sir Cliff Richard pick up the microphone and sing a number of his songs with tennis stars Martina Navratilova, Pam Shriver, Gigi Fernandez and Virginia Wade joining in as a backup vocal group. It was a memorable half an hour for the crowd, which almost felt disappointed when the sun came out and play resumed. It was later revealed that a Wimbledon official had spotted Sir Cliff in the crowd and had asked him if it would be possible to entertain the crowd with a few songs during the rain break. Ever the gentleman, he agreed!

The Most Famous Friendship in Olympics, or Perhaps Even in Sports

Friendships between rival athletes are common at the Olympic Games. After all, beneath the competition, there is also a strong element of mutual respect and even admiration. But of all the friendships forged in the Games, nothing comes close to the one between Luz Long of Germany and Jesse Owens of the United States. Although they were both competing for gold in the long jump, they could not have been more different. Long was the perfect Aryan showcase for Adolf Hitler – tall, fair and blue-eyed – while Owens was dark (referred derogatorily as a 'Negro') with African roots, a race Hitler and his Nazi administration considered 'inferior'. However, the two struck up a friendship that is legendary in the history of not just sports but humanity.

It all started at the long jump qualifying stages, when Owens, who was the world record holder and favourite in the event, took a jump in his tracksuit just to warm up. To his shock, the officials counted it as a proper effort and would not change his mind no matter how much Owens argued his case. A very annoyed Owens then fouled his second jump and suddenly found himself a jump away from being disqualified from the event everyone had thought he would win easily. Seeing him rattled, Luz Long, who was the local favourite, walked up to Owens and told him to jump from well before the foul line, and some say, even placed his towel as a marker for his rival. Owens, who had initially been suspicious of Long (he was after all, German), followed this advice and qualified easily. In the final, Owens and Long competed against each other, and at one stage, it had seemed as though Long would win before Owens took the gold with a massive leap. As thousands of spectators watched in surprise, Long and Owens walked around the track, arm in arm, and chatting happily.

Their friendship continued well after the Games, with both exchanging letters. When World War II broke out, Long joined the German army, but their correspondence continued. Before he was killed in Italy in 1943, Long wrote his last letter to his friend and once-rival:

'My heart tells me, if I be honest with you, that this is the last letter I shall ever write. If it is so, I ask you something. It is something so very important to me. It is you go to Germany when this war is done, someday find my Karl, and tell him about his father. Tell him, Jesse, what times were like when we were not separated by war. I am saying – tell him how things can be between men on this earth.'

Owens did go back to Germany to meet Karl in 1951, and the two stayed in touch. When Karl got married, many people were surprised to see a dark man arrive to play the role of Karl's best man at the wedding. It was Jesse Owens. Somewhere, Luz Long would have been smiling.

The Most Sporting Football Player of All Time

Football can be a rough sport and often sees a fair deal of fouls. Punishments for these fouls generally takes the form of a yellow card (a caution or a booking) or a red card, in which case the player is sent off the ground and can take no further part in the match. Rare indeed is the football player who can go through a year of matches without receiving either a red or yellow card. Which is what makes England's Gary Linekar so special. In a career spanning almost eighteen years and more than five hundred matches for club and country, Linekar never received a yellow or a red card! Small wonder he is considered by many to be the most sporting football player of all time.

CHAPTER FIVE

LOL, That's Sport

Treating the King with Kid Gloves

The first modern Olympics held at Athens in 1896 were notable for the fact that members of the Greek royal family attended many of the events. Some competitors were extremely conscious of this. In one of the heats (preliminary races) for the 100 metres, US sprinter Tom Curtis was surprised to see one of his competitors, a Frenchman, pulling on a pair of white kid gloves before the race. Wondering why a sprinter would want to wear gloves on his hands before a race, Curtis asked him the reason. Prompt came the reply: 'That is because I am running before the king!'

When Someone Shouts 'Fast', Stop!

Imagine having to stop when someone shouts 'Fast'? Utterly contradictory though that may sound, that is exactly what you have to do in an archery contest. At the call of 'Fast,' all archers have to stop shooting and return their arrows to their quivers.

Olympic Champ in Films? This One Did Not Say Neigh

A number of Olympic champions have made a career in films (the most notable being Johnny Weismuller and Buster Crabbe) but Cornishman V was very different. Winner of the three-day equestrian event in the 1968 and 1972 Olympics, he appeared in two Hollywood films, *Dead Cert* and *International Velvet*. Mind you, he did not get much to say. He was, after all, a horse.

The Mother Who Watched Her Son at the Olympics and Made Trainers Lose Their Clothes!

Women were not permitted to participate or even watch the Olympics in ancient times. However, in 404 BCE, Callipateira, the mother of one of the athletes, wanted to see her son perform. As women were not allowed in the Games, she disguised herself as a man and went to the Games in the guise of a trainer. All went well until she had to climb out of the trainers' area and her clothing came undone. By all accounts, she was forgiven by the authorities. However, thanks to her, a new rule was put into place at the Olympics – like athletes, trainers too would have to appear in the nude at the Games!

Current-Aided Swimming

Athletes in running, leaping and throwing events often benefit from a strong wind that's behind them. However, in the 1900 Olympic Games, it was the swimmers who got a boost from nature. The swimming events were held in the River Seine, and officials were surprised at the very fast times being recorded. They then realized that this was because swimmers were swimming with the strong currents in the river behind them!

Saved by the Music

In rhythmic gymnastics, gymnasts perform to music, which adds an artistic element to their performance. However, for Marina Lobach of the USSR, music was much more than that. As she seemed to be taking too long in her clubs routine, her pianist speeded up the music, making her go faster and ensuring that she finished well in time. She ended up winning the gold!

Tarzan to the Rescue

In 1958, a group of Hollywood stars had arrived in Havana, Cuba, to participate in a celebrity golf tournament. As they were travelling to the course, their car was stopped by Cuban nationalist guerillas. The celebrities were terrified that they would be held hostage or killed, but one of them stood up in the car, and beating on his chest with both hands, let out a long-drawn-out shout. The guerillas stared in amazement, and then throwing down their guns, surrounded the celebrity, shouting 'Es Tarzan! Es Tarzan de la Jungla! Bienvenido!' (It's Tarzan! It's Tarzan of the jungle. Welcome!). The celebrity was Olympic swimming champion Johnny Weismuller, who was also famous for acting as Tarzan!

The Heaviest Olympian of Them All

The Olympics have seen some very heavy competitors. Literally. With many sports having weight-based categories, athletes who weigh above a hundred kilograms are a common sight. No athlete, however, has quite achieved the heights of weight attained by Ricardo Blas Jr. of Guam. A judoka, Blas was nicknamed 'the Little Mountain' because of his weight. He tipped the scales at a staggering 218 kilograms, making him the heaviest athlete to ever participate in the Olympics. Mind you, his weight did not seem to help him – he lost all his bouts in the 2008 Olympics and lost in the second round in the 2012 Olympics. The US's Chris Taylor handled his weight better. At 187 kilograms, he is the second heaviest athlete to take part in an Olympics and won the bronze medal in the 1972 Olympics.

The Only Sport Played on the Moon

The moon joined the list of sporting arenas in 1971. Alan Shepard, a member of the Apollo 14 mission to the moon, actually played golf on the surface of the Earth's natural satellite. To be fair, he played just two strokes – missing the ball altogether with his first attempt and then hitting it out of sight into outer space with his second.

Want to Win in the Olympics? Lose Those Clothes!

Contrary to what many believe, competitors in the ancient Olympics did not compete naked but wore some items of clothing. So where does the belief of athletes always competing in the altogether in the Olympics come from? According to some historians, credit (if dubious) for this should go to a sprinter called Orsippos, whose loincloth came off while he was running in the 720 BCE Olympics. He still managed to win the race, which led to another athlete, Akanthos of Sparta, to believe that his lack of clothing might have played a role in his victory. Akanthos proceeded to compete in the double stade event without wearing a stitch of cloth. And won. And lo and behold, nudity had arrived at the ancient Olympics.

In the World Cup Final, but with No Jerseys!

Reaching a World Cup final is the dream of every football team. But for one football team, reaching the final was a headache as it did not have anything to wear in the final! This was the fate of Brazil in the 1958 World Cup final. The Brazilian football team was legendary for its yellow jersey nicknamed 'Canarinho' (canary), and it wore this jersey right through the tournament. However, Brazil's opponent in the final was Sweden, which also wore yellow. A draw was proposed to sort out the issue, but Brazil refused to participate, which left Sweden as the winners, letting them wear the yellow jersey. On the eve of the final, Brazil football staff were frantically searching for jerseys and managed to get 22 blue jerseys and stitched the team's emblem on them. Incidentally, Brazil won the match 5-2, winning the World Cup for the first time.

The Football Team That Refused to Wear White Because It Was Unlucky

White is one of the most neutral colours in sport and has been worn by almost every football team on some occasion or the other. Brazil, however, refused to wear white for almost seventy years. This was because the colour was associated with Brazil's most traumatic sporting defeat, a 2-1 loss to Uruguay in 1950 that cost Brazil the World Cup. The Brazilian team had been playing in white on that day, and so shocked was the country by the defeat that it changed the kit and steered clear of wearing white right until 2019!

Grand Slam Finalist, but This Bunny Is Known for Bare-Legged Brilliance

Henry Wilfred Austin, affectionately known as Bunny Austin, of Britain had a reasonably successful tennis career. He was ranked number two in the world in 1931 and reached the final of the men's singles at the French Open in 1937 and at Wimbledon in 1938 (interestingly, no other British male player would reach that far until Andry Murray in 2012). He was also part of the British team that won three consecutive Davis Cup tournaments from 1933–35 and was a contemporary of the legendary Fred Perry.

However, Bunny's greatest contribution to tennis was entirely sartorial. In 1933, Austin made sporting clothing history when he appeared on the Centre Court at Wimbledon wearing a pair of shorts instead of long trousers, which were the norm those days. Interestingly, Austin was the brother of Joan Lycett, who, two years earlier, had become the first woman tennis player to play bare-legged (without stockings) at Wimbledon.

Shutting up the Referee… Literally

Disagreements between players and referees are common in football, but they generally do not go beyond verbal spats. In the 1936 Olympic Games at Berlin, however, things moved to another level. In the match between Italy and the US, when it seemed that the German referee would send off an Italian player, the other players literally pinned his arms to his sides and clamped his mouth shut.

'Talking to Your Horse? You Are Disqualified!'

Riders in the dressage event of equestrian sport in Olympics have to strictly follow a code of silence while going through their routine – they need to communicate with their horses without speaking to them. And this rule is very strictly enforced. Bertil Sandstorm of Sweden was disqualified from the dressage event in 1932 because he was heard making clicking sounds to control his house. Sandstorm claimed that the sound was the creaking of his saddle, but the judges did not agree.

Playing Your Opponents Tomorrow? Feed Them Well!

Field hockey was a relatively small affair in the 1920 Olympic Games at Antwerp, with only four teams competing. Great

Britain were overwhelming favourites, but one of their opponents is believed to have tried to weaken them by inviting the team to a massive dinner party on the eve of a match and trying to overfeed the players. It did not work. Britain went on to win the gold medal quite easily.

The Champion Who Always Looked in Pain

Emil Zatopek of what was formerly known as Czechoslovakia is considered to be one of the greatest long-distance runners of all time. His greatest feat was winning the 5,000 metres, 10,000 metres and the marathon at the 1952 Olympics at Helsinki, becoming the first man to record this amazing feat (although he had never run the marathon before, but that is another story). However, those who saw Zatopek running often got concerned about his health. That is because the Czech ran with an expression that seemed to indicate sheer agony and pain. Off the track, he was an amiable person with a ready smile, but on the track, he seemed as if he were in a torture chamber!

Gymnastics and Gymming? No Clothes Please

The origins of the word 'gymnastics' are not the best dressed. The word is derived from the Greek word 'gymnos', which means 'naked', and 'gymnazein', which means 'to train naked'. And this was rather accurate. There was no dress code – literally – in gymnasiums in ancient Greece.

Completing a Marathon in 54 Years!

Shizo Kanakuri of Japan has a rather odd record to his name – that of taking the longest time ever to complete a marathon.

Kanakuri had arrived in the 1912 Olympic Games with what many claimed was one of the fastest times ever recorded in the marathon. As Japan did not have funds, Kanakuri had to finance his own travel to Stockholm – his fellow students at college held a fundraiser and his brother borrowed money for the trip. However, the eighteen-day trip (no aircraft in those days) was a tough one for Kanakuri, and he arrived in Stockholm in poor health. With the Japanese team coach being ill too, Kanakuri did not get enough training for the marathon. It was hardly surprising then that he pulled out from the race midway through it (although some say he had to stop after having fallen asleep following a quick snack with a family having a picnic) and is believed to have been taken care of by a local family. Ashamed of having let down his nation and those who had backed him, Kanakuri returned quietly to Japan. However, he did so without having informed the race officials. When the number of runners was tallied at the end of the race, Kanakuri was marked as missing, and for a long time, Sweden was abuzz with rumours and even sightings of the 'lost runner'. Meanwhile, Kanakuri continued running in Japan and was even called the Father of the Marathon for his excellent performances. In 1962, a Swedish journalist visited Japan on the fiftieth anniversary of the race and met Kanakuri. Such was his popularity in Sweden that in 1966, Swedish Television offered Kanakuri the opportunity to finish the race he had abandoned midway more than fifty years ago. Now seventy-five, Kanakuri took up the offer and eventually finished the race, announcing', Time, fifty-four years and eight months six days five hours 32 minutes 20 seconds 3, which will end the entire schedule of the fifth Stockholm Olympic Games.' He later added, 'It was a long trip. Along the way, I got married, had six children and ten grandchildren.' Whoever thought that the marathon was a long race surely did not plan it to be THIS long.

The Surprise Champion Who Caught the Band Off Guard

When Abebe Bikila of Ethiopia won the men's marathon very comfortably at the 1960 Olympic Games at Rome, many were surprised because they had not heard of him at all. The band at the medal presentation ceremony was equally ignorant of not just Bikila but also his country, Ethiopia, and played the Italian national anthem after Bikila was awarded the gold!

The Sport with a Kisser!

In sport, a kisser does not have any romantic connotations associated with it. The kisser is actually a set of buttons placed on the string of bows used in archery. They get their name from the fact that archers draw the string to their lips or beyond before shooting to get the best position – they 'kiss' the buttons in a manner of speaking.

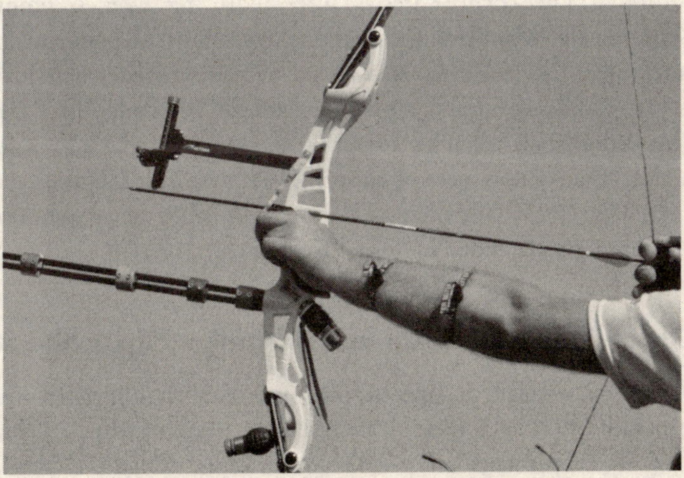

Archery

What Does the Fastest Man on Earth Run On? Well, Chicken Nuggets!

Usain Bolt of Jamaica holds the record for the 100 metres and is widely considered to be the fastest man on Earth. A finely tuned athlete, his diet and routine are very carefully monitored. However, during the 2008 Olympic Games at Beijing, Bolt was so terrified of the local cuisine after trying it once, that he resorted to eating the only thing he trusted to not make him ill – chicken nuggets from McDonald's. In his autobiography, *Fastest Man Alive*, Bolt claims he ate nothing else during the Olympics, washing them down with bottled water. As per some estimates, he ate a hundred nuggets a day and over a thousand during his stay at the Games. It seemed to work wonders – he won both the 100 metres and 200 metres comfortably. We are not sure he repeated the diet too often, though.

'Madam, Where Are Your Stockings?'

Although knee-length dresses were worn by women tennis players at the Wimbledon championships, almost all players wore stockings. This tradition is believed to have ended when Joan Lycett of Britain turned up bare-legged for her match in 1931. Shocked officials asked her to put on stockings, to which she gave a reply that is now part of sporting folklore, 'But I haven't got any.' The *Times* hailed her as 'daring' and called her a 'pioneer' even though she ended up losing the match.

Olga Flips on the Beam, and the Judges Flip in Shock!

The balance beam is one of the most challenging gymnastic apparatuses. It is a mere 4 inches wide, making carrying out difficult movements on it quite a challenge. Olga Korbut of the USSR shocked everyone when she actually did a backward somersault on the narrow beam at the 1972 Olympics, becoming the first person to do so! It has become more popular now, but at that time, people were shocked.

Frayed Tempers in Bodyline (Colourful Language Alert!)

Tempers were running high during the 'Bodyline' cricket series between Australia and England in 1932–33. England's captain, Douglas Jardine, was accused by many of using the unsporting technique of bowling fast at the body of the batsmen (hence the term 'bodyline'), causing injury. Australian players had been hurt, and spectators had been so incensed at that time, the authorities felt that there could be a riot in the cricket ground. Jardine was hardly the most popular man around. When he swatted a fly while fielding, a spectator jeered and called out, 'Don't kill the flies, Jardine. They are the only friends you have.' But even he had had enough when he felt an Australian player had called him a b*****d on the field. An annoyed Jardine stormed into the Australian dressing room and demanded an apology. This led to the Australian vice-captain Vic Richardson turning to his teammates and asking one of cricket's most famous questions, 'All right, so which of you b*****ds called this b*****d a b*****d?'

The Dog Who Saved the World Cup

A dog saved the 1966 World Cup. Literally. Football's most prestigious tournament was to be hosted by Britain in 1966. So imagine the panic that gripped the hosts when the World Cup trophy itself (called the Jules Rimet Trophy) went missing a few months before the tournament. It was stolen after it had been on public display in a glass cabinet at Westminster. A ransom note with a demand for cash (GBP15,000 – a big sum in 1966) was duly sent to the Football Association (FA), but although a person was arrested and later convicted, the trophy itself was not found. Almost a week later, the trophy was found wrapped up in a newspaper near a car in London, by a black and white Collie named Pickles. Not surprisingly, Pickles and his owner, David Corbett, were the heroes of the day. Corbett got a cash award while Pickles got a special medal and was even invited to participate in the celebrations when England won the World Cup later!

Torn Trousers, Impromptu Haircut… Cricket's Weirdest Century

Indian cricketing great Sunil Gavaskar scored 34 Test centuries in his Test career as a cricketer. But perhaps none was as dramatic as the 101 he scored at Old Trafford in 1974. Gavaskar rates the century as one of his best, but there was more to it than just great technique and temperament. During his innings, Gavaskar's trousers got torn in the upper portion of the inner thigh. There has been no official reason given for it (some say he was superstitious, some say he did not want his concentration disturbed), but Gavaskar continued batting with those torn trousers and got a century. He was run out finally, and we wonder if those torn trousers had a role in that. That was not all. During the innings, he got fed up of his hair getting in his eyes and asked the umpire to cut it. In short, he remains the only player to have scored a Test hundred after getting a haircut in the middle of the pitch and while wearing trousers that needed serious repair!

When Muhammad Ali Fooled the World

One of the most iconic photographs in sports photography is that of the legendary boxer Muhammad Ali boxing in a swimming pool. The image was snapped in 1961 when Ali (then known as

Cassius Clay) told a sports photographer that he practised boxing in a swimming pool as the water provided greater resistance to his punches and also made his movement better. An impressed photographer duly shot an elaborate photo feature that later appeared in *Life* magazine. The images created a sensation, drawing attention to the young boxer. Much later, Ali told the photographer that he actually never trained in a pool and could not even swim. Typical!

The Cricket Match in Which the Ball Exploded... Literally

One of the strangest entries in a cricket scorebook can be seen in the book on the match between Leicestershire and Sussex in the 1960s. The scorer notes that no runs were scored off a particular delivery and adds two words: 'ball exploded'. Well, it actually did. As the match was getting a little dull, Sussex pace bowler John Snow ran in and bowled a bouncer at batsman Peter Marner. Marner hit the ball and was shocked to see it shatter into pieces. Snow had bowled a ball made of soap as a prank!

Tunnelling in to Watch a Football Match

We have heard of prisoners digging tunnels to get out of prison. However, such was the interest in the football final of the 1920 Olympic Games between hosts Belgium and Czechoslovakia that many actually dug a tunnel that opened into the stadium. It allowed thousands of fans to get into the match free of cost, severely straining the capacity of an already packed stadium!

Women Are Allowed Music, but Men Are Not

One of the few gymnastic events that both men and women have in common are the floor exercises. But even here, there are differences. Women are allowed to go through their routines to the accompaniment of music, while the men have no such option. Interestingly, women's floor exercises are longer and can be between 70–90 seconds, while men have a limit of 60–70 seconds.

An Elephant on a Cricket Ground!

There are numerous instances of animals running onto the field of play in different sports, but in 1971, spectators at the Oval cricket ground in England, following a Test match between India and England, were treated to a very rare sight – an elephant was walking around the ground. The elephant, called Bella, actually belonged to the Chessington Zoo and had been brought to the ground by Indian supporters. India had a good chance of winning a Test match for the very first time ever in England, and cricket supporters had brought the elephant to the ground to mark the Indian festival of Ganesh Chaturthi (celebrated in honour of an elephant-headed god) to bring good fortune to the team. It did not seem to work initially as the Indian captain, Ajit Wadekar, was out the moment play began, but India eventually went on to win the match and create history. Perhaps Bella deserves some credit!

The Only Sports That Exist, According to Ernest Hemingway

Legendary literary figure and Nobel Prize winner Ernest Hemingway was an ardent sports lover. But he had some pretty strict ideas about what constituted sport and what did not. In fact, he considered only three sports to be truly sports. These were:

- Bullfighting
- Motor Racing
- Mountaineering

All the rest, according to this great author, 'are merely games'. None of these sports are in the Olympics, interestingly.

Javelin Throws Are Dangerous for… Spectators

Athletes became so good in the javelin throw in the 1980s that the javelins thrown by them started landing on the track surrounding the throwing area and even raised concerns of them landing in the crowd. When a javelin thrower actually threw the javelin more than 100 metres in 1984, the authorities got so worried about potential injury to athletes and spectators that they changed the design specifications of the javelin in 1986 to ensure that it plunged to the ground earlier, reducing the distance it could be thrown significantly. Javelin throw distances have come down drastically with 90 metres now being a rarity. Neeraj Chopra, India's world and Olympic champion, has a best of 89.94 metres at the time of writing.

Going on a Holiday, Winning a Gold Medal

Winning an Olympic gold medal is associated with careful preparation and a lot of hard work and practice these days. The first Olympic tennis champion, however, had none of these. John Boland of Ireland had arrived in Athens in 1896 on a holiday trip. Hearing that the Olympic Games were going on, he entered his name for the tennis event – no, there was nothing known as qualifying – and actually ended up winning both the singles and doubles events!

That Sinking Feeling… In The Boat Race

The race between the boat clubs of Oxford and Cambridge University is so legendary that it is literally called The Boat Race.

The race has been taking place every year since 1856, interrupted only by wars and calamities. In 1912, however, the race faced one of its most intriguing challenges when the Cambridge boat sank and the Oxford boat was too waterlogged to carry on. The race was declared a 'no race' and are row was scheduled for the next day, which happened to be 1 April! Oxford won for the record, but it remains the only time both races in The Boat Race were unable to finish.

The Olympic Champ Who Was Checked for Her Gender and Asked for a Date by Hitler

It was a very busy Olympic Games for 18-year-old Helen Stephens at Berlin in 1936. Nicknamed the Fulton Flash for her speed in the sprints, she won the 100 metres and the 4x100m relay at the Games. But that was not all. A tall girl, she was accused of being a man by one of her rivals and had to undergo a physical examination to confirm that she was a woman. German leader Adolf Hitler seemed to have no such doubts about her femininity. According to Stephens, she was 'pinched' by Hitler, who then asked her to spend the weekend with him. She refused.

The Craziest Marathon Runner Ever

Marathons can often attract some very odd participants, but none could have been as eccentric as Felix Carvajal of Cuba. He arrived at the 1904 Olympics to compete in the marathon, but he lost all his money at gambling and had to hitchhike and walk his way from New Orleans to St. Louis. He arrived at the marathon in his street clothes and cut his trousers at the knees to make them more comfortable for running. He was easily the most entertaining runner of the event, stopping and chatting with spectators, and even grabbing some apples from an orchard (which made him feel ill). He even claimed to have taken a short nap when he felt unwell. The amazing part? He still finished fourth!

Winning the Marathon after Taking a Lift!

The marathon event of the 1904 Olympics was run in very warm and dusty conditions. The first man to cross the finish line was Fed Lorz of the US. However, as he was about to be awarded the medal (he had already posed for a photograph with the daughter of the US president), it emerged that he had actually taken a lift in a car for almost 11 miles and started running again. Lorz claimed that it was all just a 'practical joke' but the Amateur Athletic Union did not see the funny side of it and banned him for life. Mind you, the ban was quickly lifted, and Lorz even won the Boston Marathon the next year, this time without any vehicular assistance!

Kayaking Upside Down… And Impressing a Gold Medallist!

Not many athletes have turned in the sort of performance that Gilda Montenegro of Costa Rica did in the women's kayak slalom in the 1992 Olympics at Barcelona. Clearly struggling with the boat, Montenegro spent a large part of her attempts upside down in the water, damaging her helmet. It was later revealed that she had not trained for the event until a month before the Olympics. The Costa Rica coach had discovered that the country had an additional berth at the Games and offered it to Montenegro. She had never been in a kayak and was in fact a rafting guide! To her credit, Montenegro took the sport seriously and qualified and did better at the next Olympic Games at Atlanta. One of those impressed by her courage was the winner of the men's single slalom, Oliver Fix of Germany. They got married later on. If you fail, try again… and again.

The Eskimo Roll!

One of the most spectacular moves in kayaking is when a kayak capsizes but is then turned right side up again by its occupants, without moving from their seats. The occupants hold their paddles out on one side of the capsized kayak (they themselves are under the water, it must be kept in mind) and push down into the water with their other arm, keeping the paddle steady. This generally results in the kayak coming back to its right side. It is known as the eskimo roll as it was a method actually used by eskimos while hunting.

Promising to Run Naked in the Streets if She Won… And Then Winning

When the US won the women's football gold medal in the 1996 Games at Atlanta, their goalkeeper had reason to both celebrate and be worried. Brianna Scurry had (rather unwisely in retrospect) told a journalist that she would run naked through the streets of Athens in Georgia if the US won gold. She was duly reminded of her promise and fulfilled it by running without any clothes for a short time in a deserted side street late in the night after her team's victory.

The Terrifying Goalkeepers

Hockey can be a dangerous sport, whether you are playing it on the ground or on ice. It is, after all, played with a hard ball or a puck that can travel at speeds of over 100 kmph. Getting hit can be painful. It is therefore common to see goalkeepers in hockey wear masks or helmets to protect their faces. In field hockey in the 1970s, some players found the masks to be actually scary, leading to them being replaced by more conventional helmets. In ice hockey, helmets and masks are used, but goalkeepers in some leagues are allowed to use any design on them. So you have *Jaws* and Halloween-inspired helmets/masks that do not just protect the head of the wearer but also scare those who see them. No, we do not know if it really works!

The Officials? Zebras!

In American football, the referees and other officials frequently wear black and white striped uniforms. Small wonder they are referred to as 'zebras'.

Shooting Cardboard Deer at the Olympics

From 1908 to 1948, the Olympics had an event called Running Deer Shooting. Fortunately, it did not involve shooting live deer. Contestants instead aimed at deer-shaped cutouts that were made of either wood or cardboard, which were moved across a distance of 75 feet.

Rhythmic Gymnastics' Strict Dress Code

Rhythmic gymnastics comes with one of the most strict dress codes of any sport. Outfits (and apparatus) cannot be gold, silver or bronze in colour. There are rules not only for the pattern and material of leotards worn by competitors, but even for necklines and the cut of the legs. Judges can cut points for jewellery and even for non-matching hairbands.

Rhythmic Gymnastics

Hitting the Bullseye and Losing!

Hitting the bullseye is the ultimate feat in shooting. But it does not always pay. In fact, hitting the bullseye cost Matthew Emmons of the US the gold medal at the 2004 Olympic Games. Going into the final round, Emmons was leading in the men's 50 metres rifle, triple position, and seemed to have won the event when his final shot hit the bullseye. Imagine his shock when he was given no points for it, and as a result, did not even get a medal. The reason was simple – he had indeed hit the bullseye, but the target had been that of his opponent! He hit the bullseye on the wrong target.

The Weightlifter Whose Problem Was… His Arms!

He was under five feet in height, but Joe DePietro of the US was far ahead of the competition in the bantamweight category of weightlifting in the 1948 Olympics. He ended up winning by a margin of more than 10 kilograms. However, it was not easy for him. The reasons were the very limbs that helped him – his arms. Although immensely strong, DePietro's arms were very short, and his biggest worry was getting the bar above his head.

Never Haggle with an Olympic Champ

An Olympic and world wrestling champion, Aleksandr Karelin was very careful about what he ate. And he ate a fair bit too, as he weighed 130 kilograms and participated in the super heavyweight wrestling category. So, when he ordered a refrigerator, it was a large one that weighed almost 400 lbs (about 180 kg). However, when it arrived, the delivery person was unable to get it to Karelin's flat, which was on the eighth floor. Karelin shrugged, picked up the refrigerator and carried it eight floors to his flat!

Going into Gymnastics? Tie up That Hair!

In gymnastics, you are supposed to keep your hair tightly tied up, whether in a braid or a bun. Some gymnastic judges even deduct points if a contestant's hair is unruly!

The Beachball That Scored a goal in a Football Match

Football has seen its share of odd goals, but none of them has been as bizarre as Darren Bent's goal for Sunderland against Liverpool in 2009. Bent kicked the ball towards the Liverpool goal, but Liverpool goalkeeper Pepe Reyna seemed to be all set to save it when the ball was suddenly deflected by a beach ball, which had been thrown on to the ground by a spectator. Much to the shock of everyone, the goal was allowed to stand and has gone down in folklore as the 'beachball goal'.

The Strangest Tennis Player of All Time

Arthur Larsen was one of the world's leading male tennis player in the 1950s, winning the 1950 US Open singles title and being a finalist at the French Open in 1954. However, he also enjoys the rather dubious reputation of being one of the strangest athletes of all time. Every match he played was riddled with superstitions, so much so that in modern times he would undoubtedly have been asked to see a therapist. His nickname was 'Tappity', and this was because he would end up tapping the baseline, the net cord, his foot or even the match official and his opponent a certain number of times during a match, depending on what he felt was 'lucky' on that day. As if that were not enough, Larsen was also often heard talking – to an invisible and imaginary eagle that was perched on his shoulder. He was not averse to talking to the crowd while playing a point and sometimes would even announce the kind of shot he was going to play before he played it, much to the consternation of his opponents. Many South American spectators called him 'El Loco'. or 'the mad one'. Larsen's explanation for his behaviour was that when he was in the army, many of his friends around him were killed while he survived. He said he felt he must have done something that day to have been lucky enough to have survived. So he tried to remember everything that day and repeat it to stay lucky. He survived the war, and that only made him more superstitious. 'The trouble is that I have so many superstitions now I sometimes forget them and that worries me even more,' he admitted once.

'Who Wants Some Piss?': The Boxing Champ Whose Biggest Challenge Came After the Fight

Chris Finnegan of Great Britain, was overcome with emotion when he won the gold medal in the middleweight boxing category in the 1968 Olympic Games at Mexico. The 24-year-old bricklayer blubbered and wept on the podium as he was awarded the gold medal, after a very close bout with Aleksei Kiselyov of the erstwhile USSR. But the challenge posed by Kiselyov in the ring was nothing compared to what Finnegan had to encounter after the bout. He had to provide a urine sample for drug testing, and that was easier said than done, because as he himself admitted later, 'If there's one thing I've never been able to do, it's have a piss while someone's watching me. I can never stand at those long urinals you get in gents' bogs, with all the other blokes having a quick squint'. So he could not provide an adequate sample. He tried drinking plenty of beer, but even that did not work. As he gave interviews after his victory, he was literally being followed around by Olympic officials carrying the sample collection equipment. They even accompanied him to a celebratory dinner. At long last, at almost 2 am, a shout rang out in the Olympic Village: 'Who wants some piss?'. Finnegan was finally ready to deliver, much to his own relief and those of the tireless and tense officials who had been following him. The test came out negative, and all was well!

Never Try to Keep out a Hurdling Champ!

In the 1930s, a well-dressed man was trying to enter a stadium through the main gate. The officials, however, said that as he was carrying a competitor's ticket, he would have to go around the stadium and enter from a different gate. The man paused, then fixed the bowler hat on his head more firmly, and holding his attaché case, ran towards the four foot gate, and then in one smooth motion, hurdled it and continued running into the stadium, even as the officials watched in astonishment. They would have been more careful if they had known that the man to whom they were denying entry was David George Brownlow Cecil, better known as Lord Burghley, the 400 meters hurdles champion at the 1928 Olympic Games, and one of the legends of the sport.

CHAPTER SIX

When Tragedy Struck

Playing Tennis Can Be Fatal, Even if You Were the First Tennis Player Ever!

The origins of tennis lie in France. And they are royal origins too. In fact, the first recorded player of the sport is none other than French monarch Louis X (1289–1316). The game in those days was called 'Jeu de Paume' or 'game of the palm' and was played initially with gloved hands before racquets made their appearance. Louis was an enthusiastic player of this sport, and being a royal helped. For instance, when he did not like playing outdoors, he had the first indoor courts made for the sport. However, the sport might have played a role in his rather untimely death. It is said that after a rather hectic session of the game at Vincennes in 1316, Louis cooled off by guzzling a rather large amount of wine and died of pneumonia or pleurisy. Some did suspect foul play too. Rather intriguingly, a very similar fate befell Francis III, the son of Francis I (the then king of France), and the Duke of Brittany. In 1525, he played a rather tiring tennis match and refreshed himself with a cool drink. Bad idea. He died shortly afterwards.

When Terrorism Hit the Olympics

There were many great sporting performances in the 1972 Olympic Games hosted by Munich. However, the Games will always be remembered for the terrorist attack in which many athletes lost their lives. On 5 September, terrorists from a Palestinian group called Black September attacked the part of the Olympic village where Israeli athletes were staying. The group killed two athletes and took nine others hostage and asked the German authorities to release certain prisoners in exchange for them. The authorities tried to rescue the hostages in a special commando operation, but things went horribly wrong, with all nine athletes who had been held hostage perishing. The event led to the boosting of security at major sporting events and is still remembered as the Munich Massacre, one of the most tragic events in the history of sport. The Israeli government is believed to have tracked and executed all the terrorists involved in the event, inspiring the Steven Spielberg film *Munich*.

Killed for a Self-Goal!

Colombia had entered the 1994 World Cup as one of the dark horses for the title, having played some impressive football in the matches leading up to the tournament, including a shock 5-0 win over Argentina in Buenos Aires. However, the team got off to a shaky start, suffering a 3-1 defeat against Romania. Then, in one of the biggest upsets of the tournament, Colombia lost 2-1 to the hosts, the US. The defeat effectively knocked the team out of the World Cup. One of the players that many blamed for the defeat against the US was Colombian defender Andre Escobar, who had accidentally deflected the ball into his own goal to give the US the lead. Five days after the Colombian team returned home after its early exit, Escobar got into an argument with some people in the parking lot of a night club in Medellin. Before onlookers realized what was happening, two of the people arguing with Escobar pulled out guns and shot him six times, shouting, 'Goal!' after every shot. They then drove away, leaving Escobar bleeding on the ground. He was taken to the hospital but could not recover and passed away. It is widely believed that Escobar's own goal on the football field cost him his life.

When Football Started a War

A football match is believed to have sparked a war in 1969. The nations involved were the neighbouring countries of Honduras and El Salvador. Although tensions had been high between the two countries, a series of football matches put them well and truly on the warpath. The matches were to qualify for the 1970 World Cup. Three matches would be played – one in each country and one in a neutral venue (Mexico in this case) – and the team that came out on top in the best of three would go through to the tournament. Honduras hosted the first match and won it, but it was an ill-tempered encounter, and trouble was very much in the air. El Salvador won the second match, which witnessed crowd disturbance. With the media on both sides further aggravating the situation, Honduras broke off diplomatic relations with El Salvador on the day of the deciding match in Mexico. El Salvador won, and less than a month later, the two nations were at war with each other. The football match was not the only reason for the war, but is believed by many to have been the catalyst for it!

When Football Counted Its Dead before a Final

The 1985 European Cup football tournament was won by Juventus of Italy, who defeated Liverpool of England by a single goal in a closely contested final at Heysel. However, the match is remembered more for the tragedy that occurred before it. A few hours before the final, there was trouble in the packed stadium, with fans of both teams throwing objects at each other. Things got out of control quickly, and fences designed to hold opposing fans apart were torn down. Many Juventus fans who were running away from charging Liverpool fans were crushed against a wall, which then collapsed. Thirty-nine people died and 600 were injured in the riot, and while the players did not want to play the match, the authorities insisted that it go ahead. It was played even as the city was placed in a state of siege. The incident led to English clubs and fans being banned from Europe for six years as Liverpool fans were seen to be at fault, and fourteen of them were found guilty of manslaughter and sentenced to imprisonment.

Disaster at Monza

It might have more safety measures than before, but Formula One racing remains a very dangerous sport. The chances of accidents occurring when cars are travelling at high speeds and are full of highly combustible fuel are very high. A number of drivers have lost their lives in accidents during Formula One races. But it was not just the drivers who were in danger during the Italian Grand Prix at Monza in 1961. Wolfgang von Trip of Germany was one of the favourites to win the race and even the World Championship, which he was leading, and was putting in a strong performance. However, at one of the curves, Trips's Ferrari crashed into the Lotus of Jim Clark and then rode up an embankment before crashing into a fence packed with spectators. Fifteen spectators died, as did the 33-year old von Trip in one of the deadliest accidents seen in modern sport.

A Football Career Ended by a Dog

Injury is a constant danger in the life of a football player. However, Chic Brodie, the goalkeeper of Brentford, a club then in England's Third Division, could never have dreamt of the source of an injury that ended his career. In a match with Colchester in 1970, Brodie was picking up the ball when a dog ran onto the ground and collided with him. Brodie sustained severe ligament damage in his knee and played only a few more times before retiring because of the injury.

The Birds That Were Burnt by the Olympic Flame

The opening ceremony of the 1988 Olympic Games at Seoul was a spectacular one, full of colour and Korean tradition. One part of it, however, went horribly wrong. It was traditional to release doves during the opening ceremony, and this was done at Seoul as well. However, many of these birds went and sat on the cauldron in which the Olympic flame was to be lit. And when the flame was lit, many doves were burnt to death. Following this tragedy, doves are now released after the flame is lit, and sometimes, not at all.

The Only Time Creatures Were Killed in an Olympic Contest

The 1900 Olympic Games featured an event that actually involved killing living beings. This was the Live Pigeon Shooting event. Leon de Lunden of Belgium won the title, shooting 21 pigeons. The event was discontinued after this.

When Fencing Turned Fatal

Fencing is contested with swords, with opponents wearing protective clothing and masks to protect their bodies and faces. However, this has not prevented accidents from taking place. The most (in)famous of these was in the 1982 World Fencing Championships in Rome when the current Olympic champion, Vladimir Smirnov, died when his opponent, Matthias Behr's foil's blade broke and its jagged edge went through the mesh of his mask and into his eye.

The Champion Who Was Stabbed by the Fan of a Rival

One of the most shocking events in the history of sport happened on 30 April 1993. The top ranked women's tennis player in the world, Monica Seles, was actually stabbed in the back while she was sitting and having a drink during a changeover. The injury and the trauma associated with it kept her out of the game for more than a year. The man arrested for attacking her was a German called Gunter Parche, who said he had stabbed Seles so that his own favourite player, Steffi Graf, would become number one. Sad to say, he succeeded. Seles was never the same player again.

The Pilot Error That Wiped Out a Football Team

The Ghana football team in 1993 was considered to be among the best not just in the African continent but in the world. Many were expecting it to make a major impact in the 1994 World Cup. On 27 April, the Ghana team took off from Libreville in Gabon to play a World Cup qualifying match against Senegal. The aircraft they were flying in developed engine trouble, and the pilot, by mistake, switched off the wrong engine. The plane plunged into the Atlantic Ocean, killing all thirty people on board. This included eighteen football players, the coach and support staff.

The Greatest Football Team That Never Was

When naming great football teams, most people mention sides like the Brazilian team of 1970, the Hungarian side of 1954, the Dutch side of 1974 and 1978 and a number of club sides like the Liverpool team of 1975–85, the Barcelona team from 2005–2016, the Ajax team of the early 1970s and so on. Many experts, however, feel that the greatest team of them all could have been the Manchester United team of the late 1950s. Nicknamed the Busby Babes because they were so young (an average age that was between twenty-one and twenty-two) and managed by Matt Busby, the team won the English league in 1955–56 and 1956–57 and seemed set to dominate football for at least a decade, given that its players were so young. However, that was fated never to happen as eight of the players perished in an air crash in Munich in February 1958 while returning from a European Cup match. Manchester United did go on to win the European Cup in 1968 with a new side, but the dream of dominating football was not realized.

The Driver Who won the Formula One Championship… After His Death

Jochen Rindt has a special place in Formula One history. A fearless driver known for stretching his cars to the limit, the 28-year-old Rindt was the favourite to win the Formula One championship in 1970, being well ahead of the competition. However, tragedy stuck during practice for the Italian Grand Prix at Monza, where his Lotus car spun off the track and hit the guardrails. Rindt died on the way to the hospital. He was, however, so far ahead of the competition, that by the time the season ended, he was still in the lead. He remains the only Formula One champion to have been crowned posthumously.

He Died with His Shoes on and with Wax on His Body

One of the biggest Olympic tragedies took place during the marathon in the 1912 Olympics at Antwerp. Francisco Lazora of Portugal, who was one of the favourites for the race, collapsed and died after having run 18 miles of the 26-mile race. Conditions were very warm, and many believe that Lazaro's decision to cover his body in wax to stop sunburn made matters worse for him. Many feel that the wax contributed to the dehydration that ultimately resulted in his demise. Today, a monument marks the place where he fell.

Cricket's Worst Accident?

There have been incidents of cricketers perishing while playing the game, but perhaps the most shocking of these occurred in 2014 during a Sheffield Shield match in Australia between New South Wales and South Australia at Sydney. When he was batting on 63, South Australia's Ohil Hughes (a distinguished international batsman) tried to hook a ball from New South Wales pace bowler Sean Abbott. He missed, and although he was wearing a helmet, the ball struck an unprotected area under his left ear. Hughes collapsed on the pitch, and although he was operated upon, he passed away two days later. Sixteen years prior to this, former Indian cricketer Raman Lamba had suffered a similar fate. Fielding in a close in position in a match in the Bangladesh League, he was hit on the temple by a fierce shot. 'I am dead,' Lamba is believed to have said to one of the players as he collapsed. He breathed his last in hospital a few days later.

The Race Stalked by Death

Seldom has a Formula One race been as stalked by death as the San Marino Grand Prix at Imola in 1994. In the practice before the race, Ruebens Barrichello of the Jordan team was involved in a high-speed crash. Among those who ran to his aid was former World Champion and racing legend Ayrton Senna of Brazil, who was also a close friend of Barrichello. There was concern that Barrichello might not survive as his tongue had blocked his airway, but his life was saved by the prompt action of an FIA doctor. A shocked Senna went back to his practice but is believed to have broken down later on when recounting Barrichello's accident. Things got worse the next day during the second qualifying session as Roland Ratzenberger of the Simtel team struck a concrete wall at a speed of more than 300 kmph. Senna rushed to the hospital but learnt that Ratzenberger had died of his injuries. Neurosurgeon Sid Watkins is believed to have told Senna that he did not have to go ahead with the race, given his state of mind, and offered to take him fishing, but the Brazilian refused. In the race the next day, two drivers, Pedro Lahmy and J.J. Lehto were involved in a high-speed crash that sent debris into the crowd, injuring some spectators. The race resumed and then it was Senna's turn. In front of a horrified audience, the racing legend ran into a concrete barrier at more than 200 kilometres per hour. Parts of his car struck him, and he suffered severe skull fractures. Although he was airlifted out of the track, Senna never recovered consciousness, bringing down the curtain on some of the deadliest racing seen in the sport's history. Inside his car was found a folded Austrian flag. Senna had intended to unfurl it as a tribute to Ratzenberger.

Formula One Race

CHAPTER SEVEN

Against All Odds

The Paralysed Woman Who Took on and Beat Men at the Olympics

An equestrian from Denmark, Lis Hartel seemed set to create a storm in the world of horse riding when she suffered a polio attack in 1944 at the age of twenty-three. Although she recovered to an extent, she could not mount or dismount horses without assistance. Despite this, she got back to horse riding and finished second in the Scandinavian championships in 1947. When non-military competitors were also allowed in the equestrian dressage events in the 1952 Olympics, Hartel participated, becoming one of the first women to compete directly against men in an Olympic sport (there were no gender categories in equestrian events). Hartel did not just participate, she also won a silver medal in the individual dressage event, becoming the first woman to win a medal in a sport in direct competition with men. She won another silver in the 1956 Olympics.

Gymnastics with a Broken Knee

In terms of sheer courage, there are not too many who can match what Shun Fujimoto of Japan did in the 1976 Olympic Games. The Japanese gymnast fractured his knee in the floor routine but decided not to tell his medical team as Japan was competing neck and neck and next with the USSR for the team title. The next day, he managed a score of 9.5 on the pommel horse and then 9.7 on the rings. However, his routine on the rings ended very painfully

– as he landed, he dislocated the already broken kneecap. His efforts ensured that Japan won the team title, and Fujimoto was hailed as a hero. He was not immune to pain, though. When asked if he would do it all again, he replied succinctly, 'No.'

Returning from the Dead… Literally

When Austrian Formula One driver Niki Lauda was pulled out of the wreckage of his car after a very bad crash in the German Grand Prix in 1976, not many gave him any chance of living, leave alone returning to the sport. Having inhaled a lot of smoke and having part of his face burnt, Lauda was in such a bad condition that a priest administered him the final rites at the hospital. Much to the surprise of everyone, Lauda actually returned to racing within forty days of his injury, wearing a specially designed helmet, and came fourth. He almost won the World Championship that year, finishing a very close second to James Hunt. He stayed in racing

Niki Lauda's helmet, Ferrari Museum, Maranello, Italy

and won the World Championship in 1977 and 1984. Not bad for someone who had been declared all but dead.

Niki Lauda at the F1 Grand Prix of Austria, 2017

The Woman Who Competed from a Wheelchair

Neroli Fairhall of New Zealand finished 35th in the women's archery event in the 1984 Olympics at Los Angeles. But she was perhaps the biggest star of the event. The reason: she was the only contestant who shot from a wheelchair. Paralysed from the waist down following a bike accident in 1969, Fairhall took up archery when she discovered that she could not use the lower portion of her body. And became so good that she competed with fully able athletes. She stunned the world when she won the gold in archery in the 1982 Commonwealth Games, and became the first paraplegic to compete in the Olympics in the 1984 Games at Los Angeles.

The Teenaged Girl Who Outswam Men in the English Channel

Men and women do not generally compete against each other in swimming conditions. Men are also generally the faster swimmers because of their physical build. However, in 1926, 19-year-old Gertrude Ederle of the United States surprised the world when she swam the English Channel. She was the first woman to swim across the English Channel, which was impressive. But what really shocked the world was her time – she had done the distance (around 21 miles) in 14 hours and 34 minutes. This was almost two hours faster than the fastest man to have done so – Enrique Tirabocchi, who had taken 16 hours and 33 minutes. When Ederle walked up the beach after her exhausting swim, the first person she met was a British immigration official who asked her for her passport.

They Said He Would Never Walk; He Won Eight Olympic Gold Medals!

Imagine losing your parents at the age of five. And then being confined to a wheelchair at the age of seven and being told you will never walk again. Well, that was exactly what happened to Raymon Ewry. Born in 1873, it was feared that he would be confined to a wheelchair for the rest of his life after a severe attack of polio. Ewry, however, not only recovered but actually went on to become one of the greatest athletes of all time. Participating in the standing long jump, standing high jump and standing triple jump, all of which involved jumping without a run-up, Ewry won what was then a record eight Olympic gold medals in the 1900, 1904 and 1908 Olympic Games (he also won two golds in the unofficial Games in 1906). He would have perhaps won more had those events not been discontinued later on. He was never beaten in the Olympics, and his eight gold medals were the highest won by any individual at the Games until Michael Phelps broke it almost a hundred years later in 2008. Not bad for a lad they said would never walk, eh?

Broken Collarbone, and Still Riding a Horse to the Gold

Jesse Owens might have won more medals, but perhaps the biggest star of the 1936 Olympics at Berlin was Konrad von Wangenheim, a member of the German team in the three-day team eventing event. von Wangenheim fell badly on the steeplechase section of the event and broke his collarbone. Although badly hurt, he realized that if he did not finish, his team would be disqualified, so he somehow got back on his horse and finished the course. The next day, he turned up with a heavily bandaged shoulder and continue to ride in the event. He fell once again. He rose again. And finished. His score was not a high one, but his refusal to give up won Germany the gold in the event. Sadly, von Wangenheim was captured by the USSR army in the Second World War and is believed to have committed suicide in a Soviet prison in Stalingrad in 1953. He remains an Olympic hero, nevertheless.

When a Country with No Snowfall Competed in the Winter Olympics!

Imagine a country that receives no snowfall at all sending a team to the Winter Olympics? Well, Jamaica did just that in the 1988 Olympic Games. The tropical country managed to qualify for the four-man bobsleigh event for the 1988 Winter Olympic Games in Calgary. The team did not win and actually did not even come with basic equipment (which it had to borrow from other teams) but was a huge attraction at the Games and very popular. The team qualified for the 1992 and 1994 Winter Olympics too, proving that you did not need to come from a country with snow to excel at winter sports.

Considered Too Inferior to Participate, Becomes an Olympic Star

Although a superb rower with more than a 100 consecutive victories, John B. Kelly of the US was not allowed to participate in one of the sport's most prestigious events, the Henley Royal Regatta in England. The reason? He was a bricklayer and therefore considered a mere 'artisan' in a sport meant for the upper class. An undeterred Kelly went on to win two gold medals (in the single sculls and double sculls) in the 1920 Olympic Games and the double sculls again in the 1924 Olympics. His son, Jack Kelly, also went on to win a bronze medal in the 1956 Olympics. But despite his considerable achievements, the most famous member of John's family was his daughter – Grace Kelly, the legendary Hollywood star who went on to become Princess Grace of Monaco.

The Parkinson's Patient Who Lit the Olympic Flame

The Olympic flame at the 1996 Olympic Games at Atlanta was lit by a person suffering from Parkinson's disease. Visibly unwell, he seemed so shaky and unsteady that there was genuine concern whether he would be able to even light the flame. He did, of course. He was former Olympic champion and perhaps the greatest boxer of all time, Muhammad Ali, who had been diagnosed with the disease in the eighties but had still come out to light the flame at the event that started his journey to greatness. It is said that the US president, Bill Clinton, broke down when he saw Ali appear to light the flame. It remains one of the most unsteady lightings of the Olympic flame. But easily the most moving.

Never Been in a Proper Pool, Swam in the Olympics

Eric Moussambani of Equatorial Guinea had never seen a proper swimming pool until he turned up for his 100 metres freestyle swimming event at the 2000 Olympic Games at Sydney. Moussambani had never swum in an Olympic-sized pool, which is 50 metres long – the only pool he had been in was 20 metres long. He had qualified for the event through a special wildcard entry system, designed to encourage participants from developing countries who did not have access to proper sports facilities.

Moussambani struggled to finish his race, recording the slowest ever time in the event – 1 minute and 52.72 seconds. This was actually even slower than the 200 metres winning time, but Moussambani still ended up winning his race as his two other competitors were disqualified for false starts. His time was too slow to let him progress, but Moussambani's efforts made him an Olympic legend of sorts, and he was appointed coach of his country's national swimming squad in 2012.

Playing a Sport and Leading Your Team with Only One Eye

Mansur Ali Khan Pataudi was one of the most admired cricket players in the world in the 1960s and 1970s. He was nicknamed 'Tiger' for his cat-like reflexes and was also renowned for his fearless batting and leadership. What was remarkable, however, was that he did it all with mainly one eye. He had been setting batting records from a very young age and was being seen by many as a future great even in his teens. However, in 1961, at the age of twenty, he lost most of the vision in his right eye following a car accident in which the glass from the windshield went into his eye. Many felt that he would not be able to play cricket after the injury, but he was back in the sport in no time at all and made his debut for India later in the same year. He would go on to be one of India's greatest players and captains, playing with his cap pulled over his damaged eye!

Scoring a Goal in the World Cup at the Age of 42

Football is supposed to be a young man's sport. Well, no one told Cameroon's Roger Milla. He was part of the Cameroon team that qualified for the 1982 World Cup and played very impressively. He was already thirty at that time and actually retired from international football in 1988 at thirty-six, after helping Cameroon win the Africa Cup of Nations in the same year and being named player of the tournament. However, when Cameroon qualified for the 1990 World Cup, Milla was asked by the president of the country, Paul Biya, to return to the national team. He did so and was one of the stars of the 1990 World Cup, scoring four goals and winning hearts with a trademark victory dance. At thirty-eight, he was also the oldest man to score a goal in the World Cup. But that was not the end of it. Cameroon qualified for the 1994 World Cup as well, and once again, Milla was part of the team. He did not have as dramatic an impact as in 1990, but his goal against Russia made him the oldest goalscorer in World Cup history at the age of forty-two!

The Over 40 Brigade at the Football World Cup

The physical intensity of football makes it essentially a young person's game. It is rare to see a football player play at the highest level of the sport once they are past the age of thirty-five, and very few even make it to the top once past the age of thirty. Seven players have, however, played in the World Cup even when beyond the age of forty.

45 years – Essam El-Hadary (Egypt) – 2018 World Cup
43 years – Faryd Mondragón (Colombia) – 2014 World Cup
42 years – Roger Milla (Cameroon) – 1994 World Cup
41 years – Pat Jennings (Northern Ireland) – 1986 World Cup
40 years – Peter Shilton (England) – 1990 World Cup
40 years – Dino Zoff (Italy) – 1982 World Cup
40 years – Ali Boumnijel (Tunisia) 2006 World Cup

Interestingly, six of the seven are goalkeepers. Roger Milla is the only outfield player in the list. Dino Zoff is also notable for not only playing at the age of forty in the 1982 World Cup but actually captaining the winning team!

Batting Twice with One Hand In a Test Match

In cricket, batting is done by a batter who grips the bat with two hands to hit the ball and score runs. The great poet Alfred Tennyson's grandson, Lionel Tennyson, however, stunned the world when he batted against Australia at Headingley in 1921 with virtually one hand. Tennyson had hurt his hand while fielding but came out to bat with one hand and also managed to score 63 and 36 in one of the most astonishing performances in cricket.

Participating at 72 in the Olympics… And Still Winning

Oscar Swahn of Sweden has a special place in the history of sport. An expert shooter, he participated in three Olympic Games – 1908, 1912 and 1920. He was sixty-one years old when he participated in his first Olympic Games in 1908 and won two gold medals. He won a gold and a silver in the 1912 Games. When the First World War ended, and the Olympic Games resumed in 1920, Swahn was back and won a silver medal. At seventy-two years, he remains the oldest winner of an Olympic medal in history, and his gold medal in 1912 makes him the oldest person ever to win an Olympic gold (he was sixty-four!).

World Cup Finalist at 75, National Champion at 76

When it comes to longevity in sport, Australia's Bob Marshall is miles ahead of others. He won the World Amateur Billiards Championship in 1936 and again in 1938. When the tournament resumed after the Second World War, he won it again in 1951 and then at the age of fifty-two in 1962. That in itself would have been impressive, and Marshall seemed to have put billiards behind him when he moved into politics in 1965, although he kept playing from time to time. He, however, stunned the world when he entered the Australian title at the age of 1985 and then travelled to India for the World Amateur Billiards Championship, forty-nine years after he had won his first title. Competing at the age of seventy-five against players who had not been born when he had won his first title would have been impressive enough, but Marshall did more than that – he actually made the final of the tournament before losing to India's Geet Sethi! As if that were not enough, he won the Australian title again next year – it was the 21st time he had won it and came a full fifty years after his first. He finally retired after this victory.

The Armless Table Tennis Player

Ibrahim Haamdtou of Egypt is perhaps the most amazing table tennis player in the world. He has no arms, having lost both arms in a train accident when he was ten years old. It did not stop him from playing table tennis. He holds the table tennis racket in his mouth and tosses the ball with his foot. He does it rather well too – he has represented Egypt in the Paralympic Games in 2016 and 2020.

Win with One Hand, Lose Hand, Win with Other

Karoly Takacs of Hungary was one of the best pistol shooters in the world in the 1930s. He qualified for the 1936 Olympic Games but was not sent because he was not an officer in the army. In 1938, a faulty hand grenade blew up in Takacs's right hand (his shooting hand). Even with his right hand badly injured, Takacs refused to give up on shooting and started practising with his left hand. He surprised everyone by winning the Hungarian National Pistol Shooting Championship in 1939, and although the Second

World War led to the cancellation of the 1940 and 1944 Olympic Games, he won the gold in the 25-metre rapid fire pistol at the 1948 Games at the age of thirty-eight. Four years later, he retained his title. He remains one of the few physically disabled athletes to have participated in the Olympics and won a medal.

Bowling with a Broken Jaw

Bowling in cricket can be a strenuous task. Now imagine doing that with a broken jaw. That is exactly what India's Anil Kumble did in a Test match against the West Indies at Antigua in 2002. Kumble had been struck on the jaw while batting, and his condition was bad enough for him to be scheduled to be flown back to India for surgery the very next day. However, he had his jaw bandaged and actually bowled 14 overs and even dismissed one of the best batsmen in the world (Brian Lara). The next day, he flew for his surgery, but his act remains one of the most courageous in the history of cricket.

The Gymnast with a Wooden Leg and Golden Medals

George Eyser of the US was one of the most successful athletes at the 1904 Olympics. He won six medals in gymnastics – three golds (parallel bars, long horse vault and 25-foot rope climbing, which was an event!), two silvers (pommel horse, all round) and one bronze (horizontal bar). He did it all with a wooden left leg. He had lost his leg in a train accident. He participated wearing a wooden prosthesis!

Bowling with a Withered Arm

Bhagwat Chandrasekhar of India suffered from a bad attack of polio when he was just six. Although he recovered, the disease left him with a withered right arm. That did not stop him from playing cricket once he had recovered, and the withered arm (which he could use more or less normally otherwise) gave him an usual, whippy action. Chandrasekhar went on to become one of the game's greatest bowlers, and was instrumental in India's first Test victory in England in 1971.

Playing Cricket for His Entire Career with Virtually One Hand

Imagine playing cricket at the highest level with only one good hand. Pakistan's Azeem Hafeez did just that. Hafeez was born with a birth defect – he had only three fingers on his right hand, restricting his ability to use it. He, however, turned out to be a very good left arm bowler in cricket. He found fielding a challenge as he generally had to catch the ball with only one hand, and special gloves had to be made for him for batting. But he was so good that he was picked to represent the proper Pakistan team eighteen times in Test cricket from 1983 to 1985.

Playing for Five Days with a Broken Hand in Plaster!

There have been many instances of players sustaining injuries in the course of a match but carrying on nevertheless. Cricketer Abdul Qadir of Pakistan, however, has a rather unique distinction – he played an entire Test match despite being injured well before it. Against the West Indies at Karachi in 1986, Qadir was selected for Pakistan even though he had a fracture in his left hand. He was, however, considered a vital component of the team, and played the entire five days with a cast on his left, fielding and batting one-handed. He played superbly too and was Pakistan's best bowler in the first innings. One cannot even imagine the level of discomfort he would have been in.

The Makeshift Team That Almost Won a Tournament

In 1993, the Zambia football team, which was considered to be among the best in the world, suffered a major tragedy when eighteen of its players perished in a plane crash while travelling for a World Cup qualifying match. The shell-shocked nation somehow put together a replacement team, with players who had hardly ever played together. To everyone's surprise, this makeshift team almost qualified for the 1994 World Cup, missing out by just one point, and a few months later, went on to make the final of the Africa Cup of Nations, losing only in the final to Nigeria. In 2012, Zambia won the Africa Cup of Nations, and the venue, ironically, was a short distance from where the ill-fated team of 1993 had taken off – Libreville in Gabon.

Winning after Falling

Athletics is replete with instances of athletes who have lost races because they stumbled and fell (most famously Mary Decker Tabb in the 3,000 metres at the 1984 Olympics), but there have been athletes who got up after falling and not only resumed the race but actually won it. Perhaps the most famous of these is Finland's Lasse Viren, who was running in fifth place when he stumbled and fell in the 10,000 metres in the 1972 Olympics. Viren got up and raced into second place within the next few hundred metres and ended up winning the gold!

Refusing to Give in

Sport is not just about winning. Often it is about celebrating the human spirit. And the Olympic marathon has seen a number of instances when athletes who finished far behind the winners won as many, if not more, accolades than the winners themselves. In the 1968 Olympic Games held at Mexico, Tanzania could afford to send only three athletes, one of whom was John Akhwari, who was entered for the marathon. Unused to running at very high altitude – the Olympics were held at an altitude of almost 10,000 feet – many competitors struggled in the race, and Akhwari was one of them. Suffering from cramps, he fell badly at close to the 20-mile mark and injured his knee. His coach attended to the wound and bandaged it, but it left Akhwari unable to run. The Tanzanian could only limp. He was advised to give up and told that the race had already ended and people had already gone home, but Akhwari refused to give up. Limping and hobbling, he crossed the finish line more than an hour after the winner and then collapsed. He had to spend two weeks in hospital to recover but returned home to a hero's welcome.

Twenty-eight years later, another marathon runner, Abdul Baser Wasiqi from Afghanistan, won hearts at the 1996 Olympics at Atlanta with an equally courageous display. Wasiqi had been unable to participate in the 1992 Olympics because of the civil war in his nation, and when he damaged his hamstring after arriving at Atlanta, it seemed he would be unable to participate this time as well. However, he turned up for the event, and although there was no chance of his being able to compete, slowly limped through the 26-mile race. The race was over when he had barely crossed the 16-mile mark, but on he went. As news filtered into the stadium about the brave Afghan, the authorities delayed the closing ceremony, which was scheduled to start after the end of the race. He entered the stadium to rapturous applause from hundreds of spectators, and fellow competitors, many of whom lined the track as he ran the final lap in the stadium. Officials and fans made a special finishing line for him using plastic tape, and when Wasiqi staggered across it, he had finished 111th and had also recorded the slowest time in the history of the event at the Olympics –

4 hours, 24 minutes and 17 seconds. But for many, he was the real hero of the race!

Winning after Almost Dying

Days after qualifying for the marathon in the 1996 Olympic Games in Atlanta, South Africa's Josia Thugwane almost lost his life. The runner, who could not read or write and worked in a coal mine, was shot by people who were stealing his car. Thugwane escaped with a scar on his chin and injured his back as he leapt from the car. His employers paid for his treatment and rehabilitation, and Thugwane arrived at Atlanta to run the marathon. He did not know much about the Olympics, and although he had won the Honolulu Marathon in 1995, he was a largely unknown quantity. He was ranked 41st in the world, and at a mere 5 foot 2 inches and 47 kilograms, was the shortest and lightest competitor in the field. So imagine the shock of the sporting world when the little South African proceeded to run the race of his life. In the closest marathon finish seen in the Olympics, Thugwane was among three runners who entered the stadium for the final lap of the gruelling race. Then against all odds, he actually took the lead and finished first, winning by a narrow margin of three seconds from South Korea's Lee Bong-Ju. A stunned Thugwane did not seem to realize just what he had achieved, and as he did not know much about the Olympics, had actually pointed to the place where he had to stand to receive the medal. He is believed to have celebrated his victory by purchasing a CD player and dozens of CDs!

Wimbledon's One-Armed Hero

The records will show that Jack Kramer of the United States won the Wimbledon tennis championships in 1947, defeating countryman Tom Brown 6–1, 6–3, 6–2 in a one-sided final. What the records will not, however, show is the name of the person who was perhaps the biggest star of the second Wimbledon tournament since the end of the Second World War. This was Hans Redl, who had initially played tennis for Austria in the 1937 Davis Cup but then had taken German citizenship. He had fought at the Battle of Stalingrad and was badly wounded, having his left hand amputated at the shoulder. Losing his arm, however, did not deter Redl from taking up tennis again, and although he could not toss the ball up with his hand, he came up with a new style of serving in which he would have the ball placed on his racket, flip it into the air and then serve. It was totally against the existing rules, but tennis administrators were so moved by Redl's courage that they gave him special permission to use this method to serve. Although he had fought for Germany not too long ago, the British crowds took to the one-handed player and roared him on to the fourth round of the singles and the quarter finals of the doubles. Redl continued playing tennis until 1968 and went on to become the president of the Austrian Tennis Federation.

CHAPTER EIGHT

Amazing Contests

A World Record That Vanished in the Blink of an Eye

There is a saying that records are meant to be broken. However, some records last for a while, and some get broken very quickly. But imagine a record that was broken literally in about the time it takes to blink an eye. It happened in the 1972 women's pentathlon event. The pentathlon is contested over five events, and participants get scored according to their performance. The final event of the pentathlon in 1972 was the 200 metres, and up till that time, the competition had been a neck-and-neck race between Mary Peters of Britain and Heide Rosendahl of the then-German Democratic Republic (East Germany). Peters started the event slightly ahead of Rosendahl, but when Rosendahl finished the race well ahead of Peters, many assumed she would win in the final tally. The final scores for each athlete were announced one by one. Rosendahl's score appeared first, and it was a new world record. Everyone in the stadium cheered, but she had barely time to raise her hand to the applause than the board showed Peters's score, which was just 10 points more than hers, and also a newer world record. As per some eagle-eyed observers, Rosendahl held the world record for a mere 1.12 seconds, which could be a world record for the shortest world record in terms of duration.

The Miracle on Ice

When the US and the USSR clashed in the ice hockey tournament of the 1980 Winter Olympics at Lake Placid, most felt there could be only one winner. The USSR was the defending champion and had won the last five of the last six ice hockey gold medals and had full-time players, many of whom were considered among the best in the world. The US team, on the other hand, was mainly made up of amateur players, with only a handful having experience at the highest level – the average age of the team was just twenty-one. The US, spurred on by a loud home crowd, had surprised many with its performance in its early matches, including a 2-2 draw with Sweden and a shock 7-3 thrashing of Czechoslovakia, one of the pre-tournament favourites. However, they were not expected to prove too much of a challenge for the mighty USSR. As the match was played at the height of the Cold War with the US and USSR facing off over the recent invasion of Afghanistan by the USSR, the setting was a very emotional one. The USSR scored first, but against all odds, the

US postage stamp depicting ice hockey – commemorating the 1980 Winter Olympics

US fought back, and the two teams were locked 2-2 at the end of the first period. The break was marked by the surprising decision of the USSR coach to substitute their legendary goalkeeper Vladislav Tretiak, but the USSR seemed back in control and ended the second period 3-2 ahead. The match was surprisingly competitive, thanks to an energetic US team that was being urged on by more than eight thousand spectators. In the final period, the impossible happened – the US scored twice, and with ten minutes left, took a 4-3 lead. The USSR threw everything at the US goal as the hosts defended desperately. When the match entered its final ten seconds, the crowd began to count down loudly even as the US team defended for dear life. And then the final whistle blew. The US players erupted into wild celebrations at having pulled off a colossal upset. The match has since gone down in sports history as one of the biggest shocks ever and is referred to as the Miracle on Ice.

The Utterly One-Sided Thrilling Match

Tennis can be played to a maximum of five sets. Five-set matches generally tend to be tense and intensely competitive affairs, with the momentum of the match swinging back and forth between the two players, culminating in what is often a close, tense fifth set. Well, that was not the case in the match between two legendary French tennis players, Henri Cochet and Jacques Brugnon, at the Carlton Club tournament in Cannes in 1927. Cochet and Brugnon were a part of the famous French Musketeers of tennis and knew each other's games very well indeed. The result was a match that went to the maximum of five sets, and yet, was not remotely thrilling, simply because each set saw one player absolutely thumping the other. Brugnon played a brilliant first set and seemed primed for a quick win when he won it easily 6-1.

However, Cochet turned on the magic in the second set, and it was his turn to totally overwhelm Brugnon to win it 6–1 himself. And when Cochet continued to hammer Brugnon in the third set, taking it 6–0, without losing a single game, many thought that the match was pretty much done and dusted. However, Brugnon surprised everyone with a dramatic revival and tore Cochet to shreds in the fourth set to win it 6–1. A roused Cochet extracted total revenge for this by not allowing Brugnon even a single game in the final set, winning it 6–0. The final score of the match read: Cochet beat Brugnon 1–6, 6–1, 6–0, 1–6, 6–0. At 33 games, it is the shortest five-set match ever played in the history of the game and is unlikely to be surpassed.

The Game with the Shot

Basketball is an incredibly fast-paced game in which the score literally changes every few seconds. But even by those standards, the 1989 playoff between the Chicago Bulls and Cleveland Cavaliers was insane. The best-of-five match series was tied at two-all, and this match was the decider. It was neck and neck right until the last minute. And the last minute itself saw the lead change a staggering six times. Cleveland seemed to have won it when Cragi Ehlo scored to give them a 100–99 lead with barely three seconds left. Then, to the shocked disbelief of the crowd, Michael Jordan got the ball and took a shot from the foul line itself. The ball went into the basket even as the buzzer went off, signalling the end of the match. Bulls had won 101–100 by scoring literally in the last second. The shot has gone down in legend as THE Shot and is considered one of the greatest 'clutch shots' (shots taken in circumstances of extreme pressure) made in any sport and an epic 'buzzer beater' (a shot that just about makes it before the final buzzer).

India Win the 1983 World Cup

There have been many upsets in cricket, but not too many come close to what India achieved in the 1983 cricket World Cup. The Indian team came to the tournament as one of the most unsuccessful teams in history – it had never beaten a Test-playing nation in the World Cup and had only won a single match, against East Africa in the 1975 World Cup. To make matters worse, India's first match in the tournament was against a team that had never lost a match in the World Cup, the defending champions, the West Indies. India shocked the cricket world by not just beating the West Indies in that match but actually making it to the final of the tournament. There they once again faced the West Indies, which started as overwhelming favourites and seemed set to win when they bowled out India cheaply. However, in what remains one of the biggest shocks in the game's history, India came back to win the match and the tournament. There are many who believe that the match literally changed cricket as it made one-day cricket very popular in India and laid the foundation of the shifting of cricketing power from England and Australia to India.

A Football Championship Decided with (Almost) the Last Kick of the Season

Drama on the final day of a football league is par for the course. There is often the title at stake at the top and the fear of relegation at the bottom. But seldom has a league gone down to the wire like the 2011–12 season. 13 May 2012 was the last day of the season, and it began with local rivals Manchester United and Manchester City having exactly the same records – both had played 37 matches, won 27, drawn 5 and lost 5, for a total of 86 points. Where they differed was in terms of goal difference – Manchester

City had scored 90 goals and conceded 27, for a goal difference of 63. United had scored 88 and conceded 33, for a difference of 55. So, if both teams got the same result on the final day, City would win thanks to its better goal difference.

On the final day, City had to play Queens Park Rangers while United had to play Sunderland. Both matches had the same starting and ending time. It was the craziest final day in the history of the league and perhaps of football. United took the lead against Sunderland to go to the top of the table, but then City scored against Queens Park Rangers to go back on top. At half-time in both matches, both City and United were leading, so City were on top of the table. The second half saw the madness start. While United continued to lead, City conceded a goal to make the score 1-1 and move to second place, two points behind United (a win gets a team three points and a draw gets them one point). Then, shockingly, City conceded another goal to fall behind 1-2 in the match, and three points behind United. Manchester United finished their match 1-0 winners, but City's match dragged on for a few minutes more. Technically, United had finished the season on top of the table.

But there was incredible late drama in the City match. The team first equalized to make it 2-2, cutting United's lead to two points, and then, with virtually the last kick of added time, scored a goal to win the match 3-2 and draw level with United. However, as City's goal difference had been better, they won the league after having been behind until almost the last kick of the season. It does not get closer than this.

Setting One World Record after Another in the Same Event

We do not know what the weather was like at Mexico City during the triple jump event during the 1968 Olympic Games. But it was raining at the event. Raining world records, that is. Giuseppe Gentile of Italy set the ball rolling with a leap of 17.10 metres in qualifying. The next day, he improved it to 17.22 metres. The USSR's Victor Saneyev then set a third world record by leaping 17.23 metres. A third athlete, Nelson Prudencio of Brazil, then beat Saneyev's record by leaping 17.27 metres. And just when everyone thought that would be it, Saneyev ran in for his final effort – and hop, stepped and jumped a massive 17.39 metres. The world record had changed five times during a single event. Blame it on the rarefied air in Mexico! There were new world records in just about every event that involved fast running, including the 100 metres, 200 metres and 400 metres.

Gone in Ten Seconds – the World's Fastest Boxing Bout

Boxing bouts are fought over 10 to 15 rounds of three minutes each. Many fights go beyond 5 rounds, but some finish very early too, when one of the boxers lands a particularly good punch, knocking out their opponent. When spectators filed in to watch a light heavyweight boxing match between Phil 'The Drill' Williams and Brandon Burke in 2007, their expectations could not have been too high. After all, neither boxer was particularly experienced – both had fought just three times each – and neither came into the bout with a lot of hype. However, what they saw was a piece of boxing history. At least those who were quick enough to get into their seats saw it. In a scene right out of Hollywood, Williams knocked Burke out with the very first punch of the fight. At ten seconds, this remains the shortest boxing match on record. The referee took more time counting out a stunned Burke and checking if he was fit to continue than the duration of the entire bout!

The 'Match of the Century' That Changed Football

There have been many important and high-profile matches in football, but according to most experts, one match changed the sport totally, turning tactics and conventional football thinking totally on its head. Interestingly, it did not take place in a World Cup or Olympics or in any major tournament or even in a qualifying match for them. The match, which many refer to as the 'Match of the Century', was played between the then-Olympic champions Hungary and a team that many considered a football superpower, England, at Wembley on 25 November 1953. Although the Hungarians came with formidable reputations and were considered one of the finest teams in the world, England went into the match as favourites, having been beaten at home only once in their history (by Northern Ireland in 1949). In the event, Hungary hammered England 6-3, in front of a crowd that was first shocked and then mesmerized by the skill of the visitors. While the result itself was a shock, it was the manner in which Hungary played that many consider to be revolutionary. Unlike the English players who stuck to conventional positions and formations, the Hungarians were far more fluid and kept switching positions, with forwards falling back and midfielders advancing to forward positions, causing total chaos in the English ranks. Many consider this match to be a turning point in football tactics with coaches of not just England but other countries also recognizing the need to think outside the narrow confines of conventional strategies. Hungary's ability to switch tactics and positions is also considered to have laid the foundation of the more fluid modern football strategy that we see today. Incidentally, Hungary also hammered England 7-1 in the 'return' match in Budapest a few months later, essentially burying the old way of playing football and dragging the sport into a new era.

Losing by a Whisker… And Then Winning by One

Losing a world championship by a narrow margin can be heartbreaking, but then winning it by an even tighter margin can be exhilarating. Austria's Formula One driver Niki Lauda is one of the few to know both feelings. He seemed to be well on course to win the 1976 Formula One World Championship when he almost died in a crash at the German Grand Prix. Although his condition was so bad that he was administered the last rites, Lauda made a surprising comeback and went into the final race of the season in the lead for the World Championship, the Japanese Grand Prix. However, driving conditions were so bad that he withdrew from the race after a single lap. James Hunt, his nearest competitor, continued the race and finished third to take the World Championship by one point. Eight years later in 1984, Lauda (who had won the championship in 1977) again went into the final race of the season, the Portugal Grand Prix, again in the lead in the World Championship. Finishing second would win him the title. The conditions were fine, and this time, Lauda drove with amazing skill and control to take second place, just behind his nearest competitor in the championship, Alain Prost of France. The second place was enough to get Lauda the championship, but his margin of victory was even smaller than the one that had cost him the title in 1976 – Lauda beat Prost in the World Championship by half a point!

Leicester Win the Premier League

There are many underdog stories in sport, many of them revolving around an exceptional performance on a particular day, but none has the almost Cinderella-like quality of Leicester City's victory in the English Premier League in 2015–16. Leicester City had been playing so poorly in 2014–15 that they had been at the bottom of the EPL, and many felt they would be relegated. They survived somehow, and in 2015–16, the club started with the target of simply not finishing in the bottom three of the twenty-team EPL. The chances of their winning the league were so laughable that bookies offered odds of 5000-1 for a Leicester EPL win. Against all odds, the team found themselves among the leaders in the early part of the season. Even then, Leicester seemed more concerned about not finishing last, confident their run (of luck, as many saw it) would end. In the event, it did not, as even as more famous and much more affluent clubs like Manchester United, Chelsea, Arsenal, Tottenham Hotspur and Liverpool, fell away, Leicester City won the EPL title. It remains a special underdog story because it was achieved against all odds not on one day or even a week or month of unexpectedly good play but over an entire season, lasting almost a year. Most experts say something like this is unlikely to ever happen again!

Losing Because He Clipped His Nails

One of the closest races in swimming history took place in the 100 metres butterfly event at the 1988 Olympic Games at Seoul. Matt Biondi of the US was the overwhelming favourite to win the race, and for a long time, seemed set to win but seemed to be losing rhythm towards the end. Biondi still seemed set to win, but he mistimed his final lunge to hit the wall to finish the race and was beaten by Suriname's Anthony Nesty. In the end, Nesty had won by a hundredth of a second – by the length it would have taken a finger to grow in a few days. 'Maybe if I had grown my fingernails a little longer… I would have won,' a disappointed Biondi later said.

The Final That Went on and on

Cricket has had its share of thrilling matches, but not too many have provided the kind of non-stop thrill that the 2019 World

Cup final did. The match was played between the hosts England and New Zealand at Lord's. New Zealand batted first and scored 241. England began poorly, but thanks to a spirited innings from Ben Stokes, equalled that score on the very last ball of the match, although they lost a wicket in attempting to go for the winning run. As per the rules of the tournament, the match now went into a super over, where each team would play one over, and the team with the bigger score would win. Again the two teams finished with exactly equal scores – 15 – although this time it was New Zealand who tied the score on the last ball and lost a wicket while attempting to get the winning run. With both sides tied twice, the English team was declared winner because it hit more boundaries – shots that went past the boundary rope for 4 or 6 runs.

Making a Hundredth of a Second Matter

The final of the women's 100 metres at the 1992 Olympics in Barcelona saw one of the most spectacular races in athletics history. In an incredibly close race, five of the runners seem to have hit the finish line almost together. The judges had to go back and forth and analyse footage closely before the final standings were declared, and seldom have the first five runners in a race been so close to each other. The difference between gold, silver and bronze was less than a tiny fingernail – a hundredth of a second separated each from the other. As if that was not close enough, those in fourth and fifth places were also separated by barely two hundredths of a second. These were the final results:

1.	G. Devers (US)	10.82 seconds
2.	J. Cuthbert (Jamaica)	10.83 seconds
3.	I. Privalova (United Team)	10.84 seconds
4.	G. Torrence (US)	10.86 seconds
5.	M. Ottey (Jamaica)	10.88 seconds

A World Cup Won with the Last Kick of the Match

The final of the 2003 Rugby Union World Cup saw an epic finish. The match was contested between England and Australia, and fortunes had fluctuated right through its duration. England seemed to have matters well in control, leading 14-5 at half-time, but Australia fought back in the second half. Still, England seemed to have one hand on the trophy as they entered the last minute of play still 14-11 ahead. However, a last-minute penalty enabled Australia to level the scores at 14-14 with ten seconds to go, taking the match into extra time. The drama continued in extra time as well, with England ending the first half of extra time leading 17-14. Australia equalled scores in the second half, and with a minute left and the scores tied at 17-17, the match seemed headed for a penalty shoot-out. However, with 28 seconds left on the clock, England's Johnny Wilkinson stunned the crowd and Australia by kicking a goal from 30 metres to win the match and tournament for England 20-17, with almost the last kick of the match!

The Tennis Match That Would Not End

Most tennis matches generally do not go beyond two or three hours. A few get into the four and five-hour zones. And hardly any go beyond even that. So you could not have blamed the US's John Isner and France's Nicholas Mahut for thinking that their first round match at Wimbledon 2010 would be over in a few hours at most. Little did they know that they would be still playing two days later! The match started at 6.13 p.m, local British time, with Isner the 23rd seed, the firm favourite to beat Mahut, who was a qualifier. Isner got off to a good start, taking the first set 6-4, but Mahut fought back to win the next two sets 6-3 and 7-6. Isner however, levelled the match by winning the fourth set 7-6. It was now down to who would win the final and fifth. However, as it was getting dark (it was 9.07 p.m.), the match was postponed to the next day. The two players started playing the final set at 2.05 p.m. the next day.

Now, as per the rules at that time, there was no tiebreak in the final set, which had to be played until a player won it by at least a two-game margin. Quite unbelievably, both players kept going at each other and were still tied in the final set when it became too dark to play at 9.09 p.m.! They had already broken the world record for the longest match and played for almost ten hours. But the match was not over yet. The next day, Isner and Mahut came out for the third time at 3.40 p.m., and after slightly more than an hour's play, Isner finally won the match by taking the fifth set by the amazing score of 70-68. In all, the two had played for eleven hours and five minutes. The last set itself had broken the record for the longest match and also the most games in a match. Such was the impact of the match that the rules were changed to bring in a tiebreak in the final set at 12-12, which also means that this is one record that is unlikely to be ever broken.

Saved by a Haircut

Charles Vinci of the US was the favourite in the bantamweight weightlifting competition in the 1956 Olympics. But he had a weight problem, and it had nothing to do with the weight he had to lift but the weight he himself was carrying. A few hours before the event, he was found to be about 700 grams overweight! He swathed himself in heavy clothes and went for an hour-long run, trying to sweat it off, but with minutes to go, still found himself 200 grams underweight. The barber saved the day for Vinci, giving him a rather severe haircut, which finally allowed him to sneak into the weight category. Vinci went on to win the gold and repeated the feat in the 1960 Olympics. To think he was a hair(cut)'s width away from not being able to take part.

Speed Demons Separated by a Hair's Breadth

Formula One racing is one of the fastest sports in the world but is not known for spectacularly close results. Yes, cars are separated by barely a few seconds, but when you consider that a Formula One car can hit speeds of 300 kmph and can travel more than 50 metres in a second, even a few seconds can mean a fair bit of distance. But even by those standards, Nigel Mansell of Britain and Ayrton Senna of Brazil were involved in one of the closest finishes in the sport in the Spanish Grand Prix at Jerez in 1986. Senna took the lead, but Mansell trimmed it down lap after lap, so much so that Mansell's McLaren was literally breathing down Senna's Lotus as they came around the final curve. Mansell kept closing in and Senna's car's tyres were in tatters, but the Brazilian held on to win somehow by a mere 0.014 seconds, one of the closest finishes in Formula One history.

When Amateurs Shocked the 'Real' Champions

Football has seen its share of shocks, but few have been as seismic as the one that occurred on 29 June 1950. The US played England in the 1950 World Cup on that day in Belo Horizante in Uruguay. England went into the match as overwhelming favourites. This was the first time the team was playing in the World Cup, and its members were called Kings of Football as England was considered to be the best team in the world and was home to one of the most popular football leagues. The US, on the other hand, had been patchily assembled and did not even have proper domestic tournaments. Most of the players in the US team were part-timers, with 'proper' jobs in other professions. What's more, the US team's form going into the tournament was horrendous – the team had lost its last seven matches, including a 7-1 defeat to Italy and a 11-0 drubbing at the hands of Norway. Small wonder that going into the match against England, no one gave the US a chance of even drawing, let alone winning, against one of the tournament favourites. Bookies had the chances of US winning at 500-1. In the event, anyone who bet on the US would have ended up making a sackful of money as, against all odds, the US team of patched-up part-timers stunned the star-laden England side 1-0, thanks to a goal by Joe Gaetjens. The English team had several chances to equalize, but nothing went right for them on the day, and US goalkeeper Frank Borghi put up an astonishing display. The match is considered one of the biggest surprises in sports history and is also referred to as the Miracle Match. The words 'Belo Horizonte' are often used in English football to refer to a shocking football result.

The Cricket Test Match That Went on for TEN Days!

Cricket Test matches today generally have a fixed duration of four or five days. However, there was a period from 1877–1939 when the concept of a 'timeless Test' was popular. These matches were played until a team won and were popular because a result was guaranteed and because neither of the two teams could simply play out time for a draw. However, most matches seldom went beyond a sixth day. The whole concept of a timeless Test, however, came to an end when England played South Africa at Durban in 1939. The match was supposed to be played until a side won. Twelve days after it had started, it was still being played with England on 646-5, chasing a target of 696. There had been nine days of play, one day had been lost to rain and two rest days had been taken. The match finally had to be declared a draw because otherwise, England would have missed their ship home!

The 'Mass Finish' in the 100 Metres

The 100 metres generally sees close finishes as the short distance of the race means that no one can actually build up a big lead. But even by those standards, the final of the men's event at the Helsinki Olympics in 1952 was chaotic. It is remembered as a 'mass finish' with all six runners seeming to hit the finishing tape at almost the same time. It was difficult to pick out the winner even through photographs (photo finishes had just come into use), and for a while, it seemed as if Herb McKenley of Jamaica had won the gold by the slimmest of margins. The judges, after a lot of photo-studying, however, decided that the gold had actually been won by Lindy Remigino of the US by an incredibly small margin – his shoulder had reached the tape an inch before McKenley's chest. Ironically, Remigino had felt that he had lost the race narrowly to McKinley and had been congratulating him when the results were announced. A stunned Remigino is believed to have told McKinley 'Gosh, Herb, it looks as though I won the darn thing.' So close was the race that the athletes in the first four places were all awarded the same time of 10.4 seconds. The photograph of the finish is still shown in quizzes, and participants are asked to spot the winner!

CHAPTER NINE

Courting Controversy

First High-Profile Transfer in Sport?

Today, it is common to see players change teams based on financial terms being offered to them. The 'transfer market' in which players and their agents negotiate moves to different teams or change terms at their existing ones are a staple part of many sports. However, this is by no means a phenomenon of modern sport. In ancient times too, athletes could be 'persuaded' to switch teams and nationalities, with just the right amount of incentive. One of the earliest instances of this is believed to be that of Sotades of Crete, who, as his name indicates, competed as a Cretan and won the long-distance race in the Olympics in 384 BCE. However, he was then 'bribed' by the Ephesians and appeared at the next Olympics in 380 BCE as a citizen of Ephesos. The Cretans were not amused and exiled him.

The Olympics Race with Just One Runner

There have been a number of odd sports events, but nothing matches the 400 metres final at the 1908 Olympics in London in terms of sheer weirdness. This was a race with only one participant, Wyndham Halswelle. Yes, the entire race consisted of one person running on the track. There was no one else – no silver or bronze medals. It was not meant to be like this, though. The final of the event featured four athletes – Wyndham Halswelle from Britain and three runners from the US: John Carpenter, William Robbins and John Taylor. At that time, the track was not divided into lanes, and it was common to see runners get in each other's way. In the US, runners were actually even allowed to obstruct their rivals on the track to an extent. This led to a lot of confusion in the final with Carpenter seeming to use his elbows to stop Halswelle from going past him. There was pandemonium in the stadium as Halswelle was the local favourite. The race was declared void and Carpenter was disqualified. However, his fellow countrymen refused to participate in the rerun of the race. That left Halswelle as the sole participant. Two days after the original race, a very reluctant Halswelle again ran the final. On an empty track, with no opponents.

The Fencer with the Tampered Sword

One of the most outrageous examples of foul play in sport came during the 1976 Olympics. It occurred during the Modern Pentathlon, which comprises five sports – fencing, swimming,

Modern Pentathlon

equestrian, shooting and cross-country running. In the fencing event, the British team protested that Boris Onischenko's épée sword was registering hits even though it was nowhere near the opponent. When Onischenko's weapon was examined, it came to light that it had been tampered with to ensure that it registered hits without touching the opponent. Onischenko was removed from the competition in what remains one of the most scandalous events of cheating in the Olympics. What made matters worse was that Onischenko was a very well-known athlete and had won gold medals at the Olympics and World Championships. This cheating incident raised big questions about those previous wins as well.

Football is 'Unsuitable' for Women!

It might sound difficult to believe, but in 1921, the English Football Association (FA) actually banned women's football teams from playing at its stadiums. The reason? The game was considered unsuitable for women and the FA believed it should not be encouraged. The ban was revoked in 1971.

When the Cold War Came to Chess

Not many sports events have been as politically charged as the World Chess Championship in 1972. The match was played between Bobby Fischer of the US and Boris Spassky of the USSR at Reykjavik in Iceland, at the height of the Cold War between the US and Soviet blocs. The USSR had been dominating chess since the late 1940s – all the world champions since 1948 had been from the USSR – while the US had a modest track record in the game. However, the face-off between a US and USSR player for the title of world champion was the perfect fuel for a media and political storm. Both players came under immense stress, and there were no end of conspiracy theories and controversies before Fischer finally won the series of matches. The encounter has spawned a number of books, as well as a musical by Tim Rice (*Chess*) and a film called *Pawn Sacrifice*.

The Most Controversial Award Ceremony of Them All

The men's 200 metres at the 1968 Olympic Games resulted in perhaps the most controversial and talked-about awards ceremony in sports history. Tommy Smith of the US won the race in a world record 19.80 seconds, with Australia's Peter Norman coming second and John Carlos of the US coming third. As they received their medals, many noted that the two Americans had come wearing only socks on their feet without their shoes. After they received their medals, the duo shocked the world by raising their fists while keeping their heads bowed as the US national anthem was played. Smith and Carlos would later say that they came shoeless to represent Black poverty, while their raised fists were seen as a Black Power salute, a sign of protest against the treatment of Black citizens in the US. Although both were booed by the crowd and were expelled from the Games, their protest is considered to be the greatest political statement ever made in the sporting arena.

When Women Were Considered Too Weak to Run 800 Metres!

Today, there are minor differences in the running events of men and women in athletics. However, women were not allowed to run races of more than 400 metres in the Olympics from 1932 to 1956. This was because of the 800 metres race, which featured nine finalists and was ultimately won by Lina Radke of Germany, who set a world record in the process. However, the reports of the race stated that many of the contestants had collapsed and some had been unable to finish the race. This led to many believing that the distance was too great for women, who were still perceived as the 'weaker sex' in a male-dominated world. Footage of the race clearly shows nothing abnormal in the race and even shows that all contestants finished, but access to this footage was limited in 1928, allowing the print media to portray the race as one that severely tested the physical limits of contestants. Women would be allowed to race more than 400 metres only in the 1960 Olympics, when the 800 metres was reinstated.

Swimming Fastest and Finishing Second!

The men's freestyle swimming event at the 1960 Olympics had one of the strangest finishes. In those days, winners were determined by special judges who were called 'finish judges', and no replays were used. The race was a close finish between Australia's John Devitt and Lance Larson of the United States. The majority of the finish judges said that Devitt had finished first, but this is where it got messy, as the timings recorded showed that Larson had actually finished the distance faster than Devitt – the three stopwatches clocking Larsen showed times of 55.0, 55.1 and 55.1 seconds, while all three stopwatches for Devitt showed his timing at a slower 55.2 seconds. After much discussion and controversy, Devitt was adjudged the winner, and both swimmers were given times of 55.2 seconds. The result was bitterly contested, though, and paved the way for electronic timing and touchpads to decide winners.

Sacked after Getting the Top Score!

Imagine putting in a record performance? And then being dropped from your team? Even though your team won? Well, that is what happened to Sir Geoffrey Boycott in 1967 in the cricket series against India. Batting against India at Headingley, Boycott scored his highest score, a massive 246 not out, and England won the Test match by 6 wickets. However, he found himself out of the team for the next match because he had batted too slowly (he had taken almost ten hours to get his runs). Entertaining spectators was more important than just big scores, as per the selectors.

The Most Controversial Goal of All Time?

Football has seen its share of controversial goals. Perhaps the best known of these is the 1986 'Hand of God' goal by Diego Maradona of Argentina against England. However, in terms of sheer controversy over a long period of time, even that goal pales in comparison to Geoff Hurst's goal for England in the 1966 World Cup final against Germany. With the score at 2-2 and the match being played in extra time, Hurst hit a shot that went past the German goalkeeper, hit the bar and bounced on the goal line before being cleared by the Germans. The Germans claimed that all of the ball had not crossed the goal line, and therefore, England had not scored a goal. The referee of the match, Gottfried Dienst, was not certain and consulted linesman Tofiq Bahramov from the USSR. He said the ball had crossed the line and the goal was awarded. With limited television cameras and footage, there was no way of finding out whether the decision was right or not. However, the goal has been hotly debated and the subject of extensive computer analysis over the years. England went on to win the final 4-2, but Germans to this day feel that they were robbed by the USSR linesman.

The Most Dramatic Finish to a Race?

There have been many amazing races, but perhaps none has had as dramatic a finish as the marathon of the 1908 Olympics at London.

Dorando Pietri of Italy, one of the favourites, entered the stadium well ahead of his rivals but in a very bad condition. He first went off in the wrong direction and was guided to the right path by officials. He then collapsed four times on the final stretch and was finally helped across the line, with some help from the officials. The 350 metres he ran in the stadium had taken ten minutes, with a shocked crowd of almost 75,000 watching. Although he finished first, he was disqualified because of the assistance he had received from officials. His stupendous effort, however, made him a celebrity, and he received a special cup from Queen Alexandra.

A Really Divine Wind

The 1968 Olympic Games in Mexico saw a flurry of world records in athletics, especially in the shorter distances. Some said that this was because of altitude, but there's also the suspicion that many of the records might actually have been wind aided. The reason? For four of the world records, the wind speed was exactly two miles per hour, which is the maximum speed allowed.

First Drug Disqualification… Guess the Drug Involved?

Hans-Gunnar Liljenwall was the first athlete to be disqualified for failing a drug test in the Olympics. He was participating in the modern pentathlon. He test positive for… wait for it… excessive alcohol.

The Non-Olympic Sport That Led to an Olympic Boycott

Nations have boycotted Olympic Games for a variety of reasons, generally political. However, the decision of many

African nations to boycott the 1976 Olympics involved a sport that was not part of the Olympics. In all, twenty-two African nations boycotted the 1976 Olympics because New Zealand undertook a tour of South Africa to play rugby! South Africa had been excluded from the Olympics for its apartheid policy since 1964, but many African nations wanted New Zealand barred from the Games, and when this did not happen, staged the first major boycott of the Olympics. The US and its allies would boycott the 1980 Games in Moscow to protest against the USSR's invasion of Afghanistan. Four years later, the USSR and its allies boycotted the 1984 Olympics at Los Angeles in what was seen as a tit-for-tat move. Fortunately, there have been no major Olympic boycotts after that.

Went to the Olympics, Defected to Another Nation

In the Cold War era, the Olympic Games saw a number of defections, with athletes and officials refusing to return to their countries and seeking asylum and citizenship of the host nation. The first incident of this kind is believed to have taken place in the 1948 Games when the president of the technical commission of the women's gymnastics event, Marie Provaznikova, refused to return to Czechoslovakia.

War on the Land, War in the Swimming Pool Water

Tensions were high in Europe when the USSR invaded Hungary in 1956. And these tensions came to the boil in the sporting arena when the two countries faced each other in the semi-finals of the water polo event. There were fouls and fights galore, and some reports even said that the colour of the water in the pool turned red from the blood of the participants. The match had to be stopped before its end out of fear that spectators would attack the players. Hungary was leading 4-0 at the time and went on to win the gold. Later on, forty-five members of the Hungarian delegation refused to go back to Hungary.

The Orchestra That Did Not Play and the Singer Who Did Not Sing in the Olympic Opening Ceremony

The opening ceremony of the 2000 Olympics featured the Sydney Symphony Orchestra playing music. And it was brilliant. There was just one tiny detail that was missing – the orchestra actually did not play any music at the ceremony and only mimed playing. The music was pre-recorded. Something similar happened in the 2008 Olympics at Beijing when a nine-year-old girl called Lin Miaoke won everyone's hearts with her rendition of 'Ode to the Motherland' in the opening ceremony. However, it was later revealed that she did not sing the song at all – the voice was that of a seven-year-old called Yang Peiyi. Yang was not considered 'photogenic' enough so was kept in the background while Lin was shown as the singer!

When the Winner Felt He Was Being Booed

Frank Shorter of the US had good reason to feel puzzled when he entered the stadium at Munich in 1972, barely a few hundred yards away from winning the prestigious Olympic marathon event. He was comfortably ahead of the field but was surprised to hear the crowd booing and whistling, especially as there had been no dispute or controversy regarding his run. He later discovered that the booing was actually for an imposter (a German student called Norbert Sudhaus) who had run into the stadium earlier and crossed the finish line, pretending to be the winner!

Water Poured over Gold Medal Hopes? Water Poured over Sport President!

The final of the hockey event in the 1972 Olympic Games was an extremely controversial one. Played between West Germany and Pakistan, it was won by Germany by a solitary goal, ending India and Pakistan's hold on the gold medal from 1928 onwards. However, the Pakistan players were incensed by what they felt was unfair refereeing. Pakistan supporters invaded the pitch a few times, leading the match to be stopped for a while. At the end of the match, a number of spectators and Pakistan officials rushed in protest to the table at which the officials were seated, and some of them even poured a bucket of water over the president of the International Hockey Federation (IHF), Rene Frank. That was not the end of it. The Pakistan players refused to wear their silver medals at the medal ceremony and turned their backs on the German national anthem when it was played. The players were initially banned for life, but this was reduced to two years later.

The First Major Drug Scandal in Sport

The world of sport has had to deal with its share of drug scandals, but the one that shook many to the core was when Ben Johnson of Canada tested positive for steroid use after winning the 100 metres in world record time in the 1988 Olympic Games at Seoul. Johnson, whose body had undergone a remarkable transformation in the period since 1985, was found guilty of steroid abuse and was stripped of his titles. His rivalry with Carl Lewis of the US had been making headlines for years, and he was one of the most famous athletes of his time. Many feel that his being caught opened the eyes of many to the dangers of drugs in athletics, something that most people until then had associated mainly with East European athletes, especially from communist nations like the USSR and the German Democratic Republic (East Germany).

Triumphed in Cycling, Defeated Cancer… Lost to Drugs!

In the late 1990s, there was perhaps no sportsperson more admired in the world than American cyclist Lance Armstrong. He not only won the famous Tour de France cycling race a record seven times in a row from 1999 to 2005 but also recovered and made a successful comeback after being diagnosed with potentially fatal cancer in 1996 and also founded a special foundation to help cancer survivors. A very popular and inspirational figure, Armstrong was seen by many as a role model in sport and life. So imagine the shock when he was found guilty of not just having used performance-enhancing drugs himself but also being the 'ringleader' of one of the most sophisticated and successful doping programmes ever seen in sport. He was banned from cycling and stripped of all his titles. Seldom has an idol fallen from grace amidst such shock and suddenness. Today, many refer to him as the biggest drugs cheat in sport history because of the duration for which he was able to get away (the likes of Diego Maradona and Ben Johnson were caught relatively quickly).

The Olympic Event That Was Open Only to Officers

For a long time, only military officers were allowed to take part in the equestrian events in the Olympics. In the 1948 Olympics, one of the members of the Swedish dressage team was Genhall Persson, who was promoted from sergeant to lieutenant just three weeks before the Games. The Swedish team won the gold medal in the team dressage event. However, Persson was demoted to his previous rank two weeks later. The Swedish team was promptly stripped of its gold medal. Fortunately, the controversy led to the abandonment of the 'military officers only' rule in the equestrian events in the Olympics.

The Olympic Legend Who Got Banned for Stealing a Flag from the Japanese Royal Palace

When it comes to swimming, Australia's Dawn Fraser has a special place in Olympic history. The Australian swimmer won the 100 metres freestyle three times in a row in the Olympics – in 1956, 1960 and 1964 – and was also the first woman to swim the 100 metres in under a minute. However, her career came to a rather odd end when she was found guilty of having stolen a flag from the palace of the Japanese emperor, Hirohito. The emperor himself gave her the flag as a souvenir later, but the Australian swimming authorities banned Fraser for ten years!

When They Got the Height of Equipment Wrong at the Olympics

The Olympics are an elite athletics event, with pinpoint and accurate measurements. However, that does not make the Games immune to measurement bloopers. One of the worst occurred in the 2000 Olympics, when officials realized that the height of the vault in the women's gymnastics event was too low. A number of gymnasts (including one of the favourites, Svetlana Khorkina) fell before the error was rectified!

The Match Neither Team Wanted to Win

Sport is full of rather regrettable incidents when teams and players have not tried their best to win matches and have been content to let their opponents easily win or draw a match. However, the Tiger

Cup in 1998 saw a very odd sight – that of both teams trying very hard to lose a match. Thailand and Indonesia were playing the match, and the reason neither wanted to win the match was that winning would have made them play the strongest team in the tournament, Vietnam, in the next round. The result was a match that bordered on high farce, with both teams trying their best to lose, and each team actually trying to stop the other from scoring own goals! With the score tied at 2-2, Indonesia finally attacked their own goal, scored and won the match despite Thailand's attempts to replicate their effort. Remarkably, both teams were allowed to stay in the tournament, although in some sort of divine justice, they both lost their next matches to exit the tournament. The match generated a lot of controversy, and the authorities later fined both teams for bringing the sport into disrepute.

149 Own Goals!

One of the saddest sights in football is that of a player accidentally scoring a goal against his or her own team – what is referred to as an own goal or self-goal. However, there was nothing tragic in the rain of own goals in a match between two teams in Madagascar in 2002. The match yielded the biggest margin of victory seen in professional football as AS Adema beat Stade Olympique l'Emyme by a staggering 149-0. For the sake of comparison, a football match on an average sees three goals! There was a reason for this goal deluge, and it had nothing whatsoever to do with the skill or ability of the winning team. The Stade Olympique players were annoyed with a refereeing decision in a previous match and decided to protest by scoring a flurry of own goals. As spectators watched in shock, the Stade Olympique players passed the ball to each other and kept scoring against their own team. One player set a record of sorts by scoring 69 own goals. It was hardly surprising that spectators demanded a refund after this farce, which remains in the *Guiness Book of World Records* as the highest scoreline recorded in any association football match.

The 'Dirtiest' Race of All Time!

The 100 meters sprint at the 1988 Olympic Games was hyped as the greatest race of all time, but is so riddled by drugs controversies surrounding the participants that many writers refer to it as the 'dirtiest race of all time'. The race was won by Ben Johnson of Canada in a world record time of 9.78 seconds and the other participants also recorded very quick times. However, Johnson was stripped of his gold medal shortly afterwards when he was found guilty of having used banned substances. The gold medal was subsequently awarded to Carl Lewis and the silver to Linford Christie, with Calvin Smith getting the bronze. Dennis Mitchell was moved up to fourth place. However, the years that passed saw drug allegations being raised about all of them, barring Smith. Mitchell and Christie (who won the 100 meters at the 1992 Olympics) both received bans for failing drugs tests later in their careers and suspicions about Carl Lewis linger to this day. With four of the top five finishers being either found guilty of drug use or suspected of it, this remains one of the most controversial races of all time, earning it the title of the 'dirtiest' race of all time.

CHAPTER TEN

They Said It

Serious sport has nothing to do with fair play. It is bound up with hatred, jealousy, boastfulness, disregard of all rules and sadistic pleasure in witnessing violence: in other words it is war minus the shooting.

– George Orwell, Nobel Prize winner and author of *1984*, in his essay 'The Sporting Spirit' published in 1945. He was not a great fan of modern sport as it was back then and is believed to have written the essay following the tour of Britain by a team from the USSR.

Beauty varies with each age. In a young man, it consists in possessing a body capable of enduring all efforts, either of the racecourse or of bodily strength, while he himself is pleasant to look upon and a sheer delight. This is why the athletes in the pentathlon are most beautiful, because they are naturally adapted for bodily exertion and for swiftness of foot.

– Aristotles, the legendary Greek philosopher, on the beauty benefits of the pentathlon, which in the ancient Olympic Games comprised five different sports – a long jump, a sprint, the discus throw, the javelin throw and wrestling.

Kleon threw me to win the wreath.

– Inscription on a discus found in ancient Olympia. It was common for winners to have their names inscribed on the discus. Not much is known of Kleon, though.

Float like a butterfly
Sting like a bee
His hands can't hit
What his eyes can't see…

– Perhaps the most famous poem in sport, attributed to Muhammad Ali, who often recited it before a bout. However, contrary to what many believe, the lines were not actually written by him. They were written by one of his cornermen, Drew Brown, better known as Bundini, and became popular in the sixties.

Muhammad Ali

If you can meet with triumph and disaster
And treat those two impostors just the same…

– Lines from Rudyard Kipling's famous poem 'If', that occupy a special place in the world of sport. They are written above the players' entrance to the Centre Court in the world's premier tennis tournament, Wimbledon.

There are two teams out there, one of them is trying to play cricket.

– Australian cricket captain Bill Woodfull during the infamous Bodyline series between England and Australia in 1932–33. The series had been marked by a new strategy by England, which seemed to target bowling the batsman and trying to hit him, rather than the wicket. Woodfull was struck a painful blow while batting, and when the English team's manager came to the Australian dressing room to see if he was all right, the Australian captain reacted with perhaps one of the most famous quotations in cricket.

We should never have created the Winter Olympic Games… but how can we stop them now?

– President of the International Olympic Committes (IOC) Avery Brundage in 1957, reacting to what were seen as increased commercial influences in the Winter Olympic Games. They could not stop the games, incidentally.

They have come to see me play, not to see you umpire.

– Credited to perhaps the first celebrity in cricket, William Gilbert (W.G-.) Grace. He is believed to have said it during a cricket match when the umpire gave him out. A relaxed Grace resumed playing and informed the umpire that the crowd had actually paid to see him play and not to see the umpire do his duty. One does not know if the wonderfully gifted and bearded cricket legend actually said it, but it is a measure of his stature that many believe that not only did he say it, but that he actually was telling the truth.

People say that football is a matter of life and death. This attitude disappoints me. It is actually more important than that.

– Bill Shankly, whom many believe to have been behind the rise of Liverpool Football Club. A plain-spoken man known for his ability to whip out quotes for the media while retaining his earthy touch, Shankly never shrank from stressing how important football was. And this quote summed up his approach to the game – an approach he transmitted to the team he managed.

Thanks, King.

– Jim Thorpe of the US keeps it simple while being complimented by royalty. Thorpe was one of the stars of the 1912 Olympics at Stockholm. He won both the pentathlon and decathlon, prompting King Gustav V of Sweden to say to him, 'Sir, you are the greatest athlete in the world.' Thorpe's answer were those two simple words – 'Thanks, King.'

We will make them grovel.

– Tony Greig, England's cricket captain prior to a series against the West Indies in 1976. Greig had meant to say that the West Indies were a good team when they were on top, but once on the back foot, they were not quite as good. His choice of words was, however, ill-advised. The fact that Greig was actually born in South Africa, a country that practised apartheid made things worse. In the end, the West Indies won the series comfortably, and Greig, ever sporting, actually grovelled in front of spectators!

A typhoon out of the east... it trampled under its feet and all but shoved out of the Olympic stadium the 11 representing the United States.

– A Los Angeles newspaper describing the Indian hockey team in the 1932 Olympic Games after it had thrashed the hosts, the US, by what was then a record margin of 24-1!

The important thing in the Olympic Games is not to win, but to take part; the important thing in life is not triumph, but the struggle; the essential thing is not to have conquered but to have fought well.

– Baron Pierre de Coubertin, the man many consider to be the father of the modern Olympic Games. Coubertin used to believe deeply in the nobility of sport and in the concept of athletic chivalry, where athletes competed intensely but without thinking of victory. These words sum up his approach to life and the Games that he brought back from the ancient world.

The harder I practise, the luckier I get.

– This quote extolling dedication to practice has its roots in gold. That said, no one quite knows who said it. It has been attributed to Gary Player, Arnold Palmer and Lee Trevino, among others. It is believed that it was said when one player lost a bet to another, and the loser grumbled that he had never seen a more lucky player!

You will never walk alone.

– A song from a Rodgers and Hammerstein musical called *Carousel*, 'You Will Never Walk Alone' is the club anthem of a number of football clubs. It is most famous in Liverpool, where it became a crowd favourite when a Liverpool band called Gerry and the Pacemakers topped the charts with their version of it. It is also sung by supporters of the Scottish club Celtic, the German club Borussia Dortmund and also of the Dutch club FC Twente.

If they could see on my face what I feel in my heart, no one would ever fight me…

– Yashuhro Yamashita of Japan, considered by many to be the greatest judoka of all time. He won the gold medal at the 1984 Olympics.

My will to live totally overcame my desire to win.

– Alfred Hajos of Hungary, after winning the 1,200 metres freestyle race at the 1896 Olympics. The swimming events were held in the open seas, and conditions were quite bad, with the water often being very cold.

I've missed more than 9,000 shots in my career. I've lost almost 300 games. 26 times, I've been trusted to take the game winning shot and missed. I've failed over and over and over again in my life. And that is why I succeed.

– Michael Jordan of the US, one of the greatest basketball players of all time, in an ad for Nike in 1997.

Michael Jordan

You miss one hundred percent of the shots you don't take... even though there is only a 1-5 percent probably of scoring.

– Wayne Gretzky of Canada, perhaps the greatest ice hockey player of all time, in an interview to Bob McKenzie in 1983.

The quote became famous when Hollywood actor Steve Carrell's character in a comedy series called *The Office* wrote it on a whiteboard in an episode called 'Michael Scott Paper Company' in the fifth season of the series.

I will start shaving, I guess.

– Bob Mathias of the US when asked how he would celebrate, after becoming the youngest male athlete to win a gold medal in an Olympic athletics event in the 1948 Games. Mathias had won the decathlon. He won it again in 1952. We have no statement about how he planned to celebrate THAT win.

You can melt down all the medals and cups I have... And they wouldn't be a plating on the 24-carat friendship I felt for Luz Long at that moment.

– Jesse Owens of the US, who won four gold medals at the 1936 Olympic Games, on his friendship with Germany's Luz Long. Long defied Hitler's racial ideology to walk arm in arm with Owens at the Olympics, and the two became close friends after the Games, writing to each other.

No mas. No mas. (No more. No more.)

– Roberto Duran of Panama while stopping fighting in the eighth round of his World Welterweight Boxing Championship bout with Sugar Ray Leonard at Louisiana in 1980. Duran had been trailing Leonard on points and complained of stomach cramps, but his decision to quit shocked many, especially in his country, Panama. The fight is now famous as the 'No Mas Fight'.

You are now the most popular man in this country.

– King George I of Greece to Germany's Carl Schumann while presenting him with the gold medal for the Greco-Roman wrestling event at the 1896 Olympics. Schumann was the most successful athlete at the Games, winning four gold medals and competing in four different sports (athletics, gymnastics, weightlifting and wrestling).

Am an Olympic champion. World record beaten. Will arrive Tuesday morning.

– Cable from France's Pierre Coquelin de Lisle to his mother, after he had won the small-bore rifle prone shooting event at the 1924 Olympics.

Kids imitate champions. If they try to imitate Fosbury, he will wipe out an entire generation of high jumpers because they will all have broken necks…

– US athletics coach Payton Jordan when he saw Dick Fosbury's revolutionary high jump technique in which he cleared the bar head first and landed on his shoulders. Today, almost all high jumpers use the same technique, which is called the Fosbury Flop.

I don't know. I've never shot standing up.

– Neroli Fairhall of New Zealand when asked if shooting from a wheelchair was a problem in windy conditions after she had won the archery event at the 1982 Commonwealth Games. Fairhall was paralysed below the waist and competed from a wheelchair. Two years later, she became the first paraplegic to compete in the Olympics when she competed in the 1984 Olympic Games.

What is one million dollars compared to the love of eight million Cubans?

– Teofilo Stevenson of Cuba, in the late 1970s. One of only two men to win three consecutive Olympic gold medals in heavyweight boxing, Stevenson was offered a huge amount to fight then current heavyweight champion, Muhammad Ali, but refused to give up his amateur status.

Football. Bloody Hell!

– Sir Alex Ferguson, legendary Manchester United manager, after his team had beaten Bayern Munich in the 1999 Champions' League final, after being behind for most of the time. Munich had led for the entire match, but Manchester United snatched victory in added time, leading to dramatic scenes and the equally dramatic quote by their legendary manager.

Aguerrroooooooo…

– Martin Tyler, famous football commentator, made this single word one of the most famous in football history on 13 May 2012. Tyler was commentating in a match between Manchester City and Queens Park Rangers. City needed to win the match to win the English Premier League (EPL) but seemed unable to do so. Then, at the very end, City striker Sergio Aguero pounced on the ball and scored the goal that won his team the trophy. Tyler's scream of 'Aguerrroooooooo' when the goal was scored has become part of football legend and is even seen on T-shirts and used as a ringtone by City fans!

A nuclear war.

– Nobuyuki Sato of Japan, a former judo world champion and the coach of Japanese Judo legend Yashuhro Yamashita when asked by *Sports Illustrated*, prior to the 1984 Olympic Games as to what could stop Yamashita from winning the gold medal. Yamashita duly won.

11 seconds, you've got 10 seconds, the countdown going on right now! Morrow, up to Silk. Five seconds left in the game. Do you believe in miracles? YES!

– Al Michaels, a commentator on the ABC Network, during the final moments of the US's shock win over the USSR in the 1980 Winter Olympics at Lake Placid. It is supposed to be one of the greatest pieces of sports commentary.

Where were the Germans? But frankly, who cares?

– British commentator Barry Davies after Great Britain's Imran Sherwani had scored Britain's third goal in a shock 3-1 win over West Germany in the hockey final of the 1988 Olympic Games in Seoul. The comment was considered blatantly partisan but has since gone down as one of the most famous pieces of sports commentary.

Ten amazing quotes from Yogi 'It ain't over 'til it's over' Berra

Yogi Berra was not only a very successful baseball player, manager and coach but was also a literal quote machine. There is hardly any book of quotes that does not contain some quotes from the man who was an All-Star eighteen times and won the World Series ten times as a player. Not all his quotes made sense – most seemed to defy logic – but most made you smile. Here are ten cherry-picked of the Berra best for you:

1. 'It ain't over 'til it's over.'
2. 'Baseball is 90 per cent mental. The other half is physical.'
3. 'You have to give 100 per cent in the first half of the game. If that isn't enough, in the second half, you have to give what is left.'
4. 'The future ain't what it used to be.'
5. 'Congratulations on breaking my record last night. I always thought the record would stand until it was broken.'
6. 'It's tough to make predictions, especially about the future.'
7. 'Always go to other people's funerals, otherwise they won't come to yours.'
8. 'The future ain't what it used to be.'

9. 'If you don't know where you are going, you will wind up somewhere else.'
10. 'It gets late out there early.' (Referring to an early sunset.)

If anyone sees me going anywhere near a boat again, they have my permission to shoot me.

– Sir Steve Redgrave, after winning the gold medal in the coxless pairs rowing competition at the 1996 Olympics at Atlanta. It was the fourth consecutive Olympic gold won by Redgrave, who was very tired after a close race. He changed his mind, however, and went on to win another gold at the 2000 Olympics, becoming the only athlete to have won gold medals in rowing at five consecutive Olympics (1984–2000).

You are too tall for gymnastics.

– A Russian gymnastics coach to Svetlana Khorkina. Khorkina was 1.65 metres tall (about five feet five inches) and was considered too tall for gymnastics. She went on to become one of the greatest gymnasts of all time, winning Olympic and world titles!

My writing is nothing. My boxing is everything.

– Ernest Hemingway. Yes, the literary legend who wrote books like *For Whom the Bell Tolls* and *A Farewell to Arms* was a huge boxing fan. Mind you, he was not as good at the sport as he thought.

Ernest Hemingway

Man, I ain't got no quarrel with them Viet Cong.

– Muhammad Ali, the then world heavyweight champion, while refusing to join the US Army to fight the Vietnam War. Ali was stripped of the title for his stance.

Ten John McEnroe Outbursts

He might be known as a tennis legend, commentator and analyst these days, but in the eighties, US tennis player John McEncore was an absolute terror on the court. Known as much for his brilliant tennis, as for his brittle temper, McEnroe was so prone to screaming and shouting at officials and spectators at matches that he was nicknamed 'Superbrat'. These are ten of his most (in) famous outbursts:

- 'You cannot be serious, man, you cannot be serious.' (To a match official.)
- 'You guys are the absolute pits of the world. Vultures. Trash!' (To a match official.)
- 'This guy is an incompetent fool.' (To the referee about a match official.)
- 'Answer my question. The question, jerk.' (To a match official.)
- 'You don't deserve to be on the same court as me. You are the worst. The worst.' (To Brad Gilbert, an opponent.)
- 'You are a communist b**tard!' (To Tomas Smid, who played for Czechoslovakia, then a communist country.)
- 'Do me a favour and stick that mic up you a***!' (To a TV crew member holding a microphone.)
- 'That ball was on the line, chalk flew up! It was clearly in, how can you possibly call that out? How many are you going to miss?' (To a match official.)
- 'Everyone knows it's in, this whole stadium, and you call it out? Explain that to me, will you?'
- 'You can go f*** your mother.'(To a match official at the 1990 Australian Open. This outburst made him the first player to be disqualified from a match in the Open era.)

My country didn't send me 7,000 miles to start the race. They sent me 7,000 miles to finish it.

– John Akhwari of Tanzania after struggling to finish the marathon at the 1968 Olympic Games. Suffering from cramps and an injury, Akhwari finished well after the other runners but refused to stop running.

My life is worth more than a title.

– Austrian Formula One driver Niki Lauda when he pulled out of the Japanese Grand Prix in 1976 as it was too dangerous to drive. Lauda had suffered a horrific crash earlier in the year that had almost killed him, and although he was leading in the World Championship, he refused to risk his life in conditions that he felt were life-threatening. He lost the championship by just one point.

When I saw the English Test attack!

– Indian cricket legend Mansur Ali Khan Pataudi when asked by an English player on how he realized he could continue playing cricket even after losing vision in one of his eyes after a car accident. Pataudi went on to play more than 40 Test matches for India and is also considered one of the greatest captains in the sport. He did this all with one good eye.

Please do not call me arrogant because what I say is true. I'm European champion. I'm not one out of the bottle, I think I'm a special one.

– Jose Mourinho, on being appointed manager of Chelsea football club in 2004. Modesty was not one of the Portuguese's virtues. Fortunately, he more than lived up to his own words, emerging as one of the most successful football managers of recent times.

Get the ball to Michael and everybody get the fk out of the way!**

– Doug Collins, coach of basketball team Chicago Bulls, on his team's strategy in the final seconds of the 1989 playoffs against Cleveland Cavaliers. It worked. Jordan scored in the last second to give the Bulls one of the closest wins in basketball history.

Sod off, father....

– Nigel Mansell to a priest in 1966. Mansell, just thirteen, had been badly injured in a go-kart accident, and so bad was his condition that a priest at the hospital he had been admitted to, administered him the last rites. A dazed Mansell is not only believed to have told the priest off in a less than parliamentary manner but also recovered, and went on to become one of the greatest car racing drivers of all time, winning the Formula One championship in 1992.

Don't worry. I will get another one.

– Carl Lewis to his mother at his father's funeral in 1987. Lewis, one of the greatest athletes of all time, was very close to his father, who played a key role in his development. Lewis became a celebrity in the 1984 Olympic Games at Los Angeles, where he won four gold medals – in the 100 meters, the 200 meters, the long jump and the 4 x 100 meters relay. When his father died of Cancer in 1987, Lewis surprised his mother by taking the 100 meters Olympic gold medal out of his pocket and placing it in his father's hands in the coffin, because it was his father's favorite event. He won several more medals!

The Yankees hold the play,
The white man pulls the trigger,

But it make no difference what the white man say,
The world champion's still a nigger!

– A poem composed by the supporters of Jack Johnson, the first black man to win the world heavyweight boxing title, after he defeated James 'Jim' Jeffries in 1910. Johnson's victory made him one of the first black athletes to be considered a world champion in a major sport. He had won the heavyweight title earlier against Tommy Burns but his victory over the unbeaten Jeffries, who had been represented as a man who would bring the title to white America, consolidated his status and is also believed to have played a key role in race relations in the US. Johnson's defeat of Jeffries also triggered the tragic Johnson-Jeffries riots that claimed almost twenty lives.

CHAPTER ELEVEN

Amazing but True

India Won Medals in the Olympics in 1900, and They Were NOT in Hockey

When people think of India at the earlier Olympics, they generally think in terms of hockey. The fact, however, is that India had won two silver medals in the Olympic Games as far back as 1900. Born in Kolkata, Pritchard won silver in both the 200 metres and the 200 metres hurdles. There is some dispute as to whether he was representing Britain or India at the Games, but the IOC has credited India with his medals, and he was also the first person of Asian birth to win medals at the modern Olympics!

The Man behind Sherlock Was a Sport Too

Everyone knows Sir Arthur Conan Doyle as the creator of the great Sherlock Holmes. What, however, not too many know is that Doyle was also a very enthusiastic, versatile and gifted sportsperson. As a young man, he was the goalkeeper of the local football club. He played cricket and was good enough to play for the legendary Marylebone Cricket Club (MCC) and even dismissed the great W.G. Grace. He was also a very competitive motorist and rugby player and was even asked to write on the 1908 London Olympic Games, where his report on Dorando Pietri's epic marathon became famous. He was also known for his interest in rugby, boxing and baseball. The creator of Sherlock Holmes was clearly a good sport.

The Longest Drive in Golf (It Did Not Help the Player At All)

For many people, golf is all about hitting long drives that get you closer to a hole. Well, the longest drive actually took the hitter further away from his target. The record for the longest drive in competitive golf stands in the name of Mike Austin, who hit it at the Winterwood Golf Course in the US National Seniors Tournament in 1974. Yes, you read that right – the Seniors Tournament. Austin was sixty-four years old and hit a staggering 515-yard drive. The problem was that the hole was only 450 yards away, so he ended up going well past it and actually had to find his way back to it and ended up with a bogey!

Cricket Was at the Olympics, You Know!

It might be the second most popular sport in the world, but cricket is not an Olympic sport. It was included in the Olympic Games once, though. This was in the 1900 Olympics in Paris and was contested by just two teams – England and France. England won by 158 runs, and the sport went back to the sidelines.

The Enemy is Sight? Let Me Finish My Game First!

Sir Francis Drake (1540–1596) is known as one of the great naval commanders and sea explorers of all time. He was one of the earliest people to circumnavigate the Earth and is also known for his defeat of the massive Spanish fleet (called the Spanish Armada) that was invading Britain in 1588. Drake was a keen sportsperson. Legend has it that when he was told that the Spanish fleet had been spotted, he was playing a game of bowls at Plymouth. An unruffled Drake is believed to have continued playing, saying, 'There is plenty of time to finish the game and still beat the Spaniards.' He did both!

World War Legend Who Participated in an Olympic Modern Pentathlon

One of the most famous generals of the Second World War was George S.S. Patton, who led the Allied and US forces across Europe in the charge towards Hitler's Berlin in 1944–45. But before he got into the military, Patton was also a keen sportsperson and actually represented the US in the modern pentathlon (an event comprising running, shooting, fencing, show jumping and swimming) in the 1912 Olympic Games in Stockholm. He finished fifth overall.

Eight Sports Champions Who Changed Their Names

Sport is full of players who changed their names. The reasons for this have varied from political, religious or simply personal beliefs, but here are eight sportspersons who legally changed their names:

1. Muhammad Ali from Cassius Clay (Boxing)
2. Sugar Ray Robinson from Walter Smith Jr. (Boxing)
3. Kareem Abdul Jabber from Lew Alcindor (Basketball)
4. Leonard ('Len') Stephen Pascoe from Leonard Stephen Durtanovich (Cricket)
5. Metta World Peace from Ronald William Artest Jr. (Basketball)
6. Ahmad Rashad from Robert Earl 'Bobby' Moore (American Football)
7. Muhammad Yousuf from Joseph Yohana (Cricket)
8. Tillakratne Dilshan from Tuwan Mohammad Dilshan (Cricket)

The Boss of Baby and.... And of Rowing in the Olympics!

Dr Benjamin Spock's *The Common Sense Book of Baby and Child Care* is supposed to be THE book for those who want to learn more about taking care of newborn children and infants. What not too many know, however, is that Benjamin Spock was actually an Olympic champion. He was part of the US team that won the coxed eights rowing event at the 1924 Olympics at Paris.

Ten Great Sportspersons Who Are Better Known by Their 'Playing' Names

You do not get stage names only in Hollywood. Sport is full of people who played under different names from their real names. These changes were made either to simplify the names or were given to them out of affection by their fans, but in all cases, they bore very little similarly to their real names. Here are ten sportspersons who you would not recognize by their real names:

1. Pelé (Real name: Edson Arantes do Nascimento) (Football)
2. Tiger Woods (Eldrick Tont Woods Jr.) (Golf)

Pelé

3. Babe Ruth (George Herman Ruth Jr.) (Baseball)
4. Magic Johnson (Earvin Johnson) (Basketball)
5. Manny Pacquiao (Emmanuel Dapidran Pacquiao) (Boxing)
6. Jesse Owens (James Cleveland Owens) (Athletics)
7. Kaka (Ricardo Izecson Dos Santos Leite) (Football)
8. Ronaldinho (Ronaldo de Assis Moreira) (Football)
9. Isco (Francisco Román Alarcón Suárez) (Football)
10. Zico (Arthur Antunes Coimbra) (Football)

Wax statue of Babe Ruth at Madame Tussauds Wax Museum, San Francisco

The Day of Batting with an Aluminium Bat

One of the oddest incidents in sports history occurred in Perth in 1979. Australia were playing England in a cricket Test match, and Dennis Lillee walked out to bat. Only, he came to bat with a bat made of aluminium, not wood. Although there was nothing in the regulations stopping Lillee from using a bat made of aluminium, the English team objected as the bat seemed to be damaging the ball more than a wooden bat would. A furious ruckus ensued in the ground as Lillee refused to change his bat, insisting he was playing within the rules of the game. In the end, he had to change the bat (aptly named ComBat), and the rules of cricket had to be changed to ensure that bats stayed wooden. Lillee's inspiration for using an aluminium bat came from baseball, where batters were using metallic bats rather than wooden ones.

Governor General, Royal Doctor… And an Olympic Medallist

Arthur Porritt of New Zealand had a very varied career. One of the best doctors of his time, he was appointed surgeon to the Prince of Wales in 1926, was part of the Normandy Landings on D-Day, was the king's surgeon from 1946 to 1952 and Serjeant Surgeon to the Queen till 1967. He then served as governor general of New Zealand from 1967 to 1972. He was also elected president of the Royal Academy of Medicine in 1966. So why is he in a book on sports? Well, because he was also an Olympic medallist, finishing third and winning bronze in the 100 metres dash in the 1924 Olympics.

Swim to Win in the Olympics, Grab a Role as Tarzan

In the 1920s and 1930s, it seemed as if Olympic swimming champions were destined to end up playing the role of Tarzan in Hollywood. Johnny Weissmuller of the US grabbed a lot of attention when he won five gold medals in the 1924 and 1928 Olympics, winning the 100 metres freestyle twice in the process. Among those watching were Hollywood directors, who signed him up to play Tarzan in a feature film. Weissmuller was so successful that he played the role in twelve films and was synonymous with Edgar Rice Burrough's legendary jungle man. History repeated itself in 1932 when Buster Crabbe of the US won the Olympic gold medal in the 400 metres freestyle and landed a role as Tarzan, although he played the role in just one film.

The Tournament with a Special Dish

Most people these days tend to watch sport with popcorn or something snack-ish. Some tournaments, however, come with not just high-class competition but even special dishes. And none is as famous as the strawberries and cream that are served at the Wimbledon Tennis Championships every year. The trend is supposed to have been started by King George V in the early part of the twentieth century, when strawberries were supposed to be very fashionable to eat (and one of the few fruits that were available). It is believed that more than 20 tonnes of strawberries are consumed at every Wimbledon tournament these days.

Who Started That Running with the Flag after Winning Celebration?

One of the most popular celebrations in sport is that of an athlete grabbing a flag from the crowd and running while waving it. While there is no accurate documentation on when this celebration started, many credit it to Bruce (now Caitlyn) Jenner, who took a US flag from the crowd and ran waving it after winning the decathlon at the 1976 Olympic Games at Montreal.

The Rules Are Named after Him, but He Did Not Write Them (Although He Was a Pain for Oscar Wilde)

There are many who believe that boxing as a sport really gained an identity of its own after the publication of the Marquess of Queensberry Code/Rules in 1867, which clearly laid out the rules of the sport. The fact is that although the rules are named after him, the Marquess of Queensbury, John Douglas, did not actually write them. A keen sportsman himself, he sponsored their writing. The writing was actually done by a Welsh sportsman called John Graham Chambers. The Marquess of Queensberry is also known as the man who ruined famous English writer and poet Oscar Wilde, exposing him as a homosexual (something that was frowned upon at that time), getting him imprisoned and destroying his reputation.

Striking the Right Note, Putting the Right Shot – Concert Pianist and Olympic Champion

Micheline Ostermeyer celebrated winning the gold medal in the shot-put in the 1948 Olympic Games in a manner that many would find odd. The Frenchwoman gave a performance of a Beethoven concert on the piano at her team's quarters and then gave another performance at the Royal Albert Hall in London later in the evening! That was because she was not just a great athlete but a remarkable concert pianist too, having learnt to play the piano at the age of four. Ostermeyer won gold in the shot-put and the discus throw (though she had picked up the sport very recently), as well as a bronze in the high jump in the 1948 Olympic Games at London but retired from sport in 1950 at the age of twenty-eight to pursue a career in music, touring successfully for fifteen years!

Grand Slam Is Actually a Card Trick

The term Grand Slam is often used in sport to indicate a team or a person winning every major competition or trophy in a particular span of time – for instance, a player winning the Australian Open, French Open, Wimbledon and US Open tournaments in the same year is said to have completed a Grand Slam. However, the term actually comes from a sport that many do not even consider a sport – the card-playing game of contract bridge. The term in the game referred to winning all possible tricks in the game!

That Iconic Crocodile Logo on Your Shirt? It Is a French Tennis Player

One of the most famous logos in the clothing industry is the crocodile that represents legendary French fashion brand Lacoste. Well, it would not have been around but for lawn tennis. Lacoste was established by Rene Lacoste, a legendary French tennis player of the 1920s and 1930s. Lacoste, along with his fellow countrymen Jean Borotra, Jacques Brugnon and Henri Cochet, formed what many called the Four Musketeers of Tennis in that era. Lacoste was nicknamed 'the alligator' following a bet over an alligator-skin suitcase. It is said that after he won the bet, a friend of his embroidered an alligator over his blazer, and it became his trademark. In 1933, Lacoste formed a company to manufacture tennis shirts, and the shirts, also known as 'polo shirts', came with the crocodile logo on the chest. That's how the iconic crocodile logo was born. Advantage, tennis.

Lacoste Brand

The Sweetest Nickname of Them All

Like people, football clubs too have nicknames. Manchester United are called the Red Devils, Manchester City are called the Blues, and Southampton are called the Saints. But perhaps no football club has a nickname that is as sweet as Everton. Literally. The club is affectionately referred to as the Toffees. The reason? There were a couple of toffee shops that were very close to the grounds where the club played, and one of them even came out with an Everton toffee. Such is the association of the club with the confectionery that even today before every football match at its ground, Goodison Ground, a mascot in blue and white (Everton's colours) throws sweets to the crowd. Sweet indeed!

The Hawk Who Watches over Wimbledon

One of the most important members of the staff at the Wimbledon Tennis Championship is a bird. It is actually a hawk called Rufus, who patrols the skies during the tournament and keeps pigeons away. A Harris's hawk, Rufus has been keeping an eye on the skies over the world's most prestigious tennis tournament since 2008 and also has a Twitter (now X) and Facebook account!

The Club Named after a Day of the Week

English football club Sheffield Wednesday are one of the few teams in the world to actually give a day of the week as part of their name. The reason is simple. The club was actually initially a cricket club and played its matches only on Wednesdays because that was the day when its founding members had some time off from work. It was known as the Wednesday Cricket Club and was founded in 1820. And when it got into football in 1867, it was known as the Wednesday Football Club. It was only in 1929 that it changed its name to Sheffield Wednesday Football Club, based on its location in Sheffield, Yorkshire.

When Royalty Took a Battering at Wimbledon

The 1926 Wimbledon Tennis Championships had a royal participant. Prince Albert, the Duke of York (who would later ascend the throne as George VI), entered the doubles event of the tournament along with his friend Louis Greig. Albert and Greig were decent tennis players and had won the doubles in the British

RAF Lawn Tennis Championships. There was, however, concern whether the prince and his partner would be able to handle the quality of opposition at Wimbledon, and many were relieved when their opponents were a pair of veterans, a 58-year-old Albert Gore and 52-year-old Herbert Barrett. Although some thought that the opponents had been deliberately chosen to ensure the prince got a relatively easy match, the fact was that both senior players were former Wimbledon champions. Gore had won the singles three times and Barrett the doubles three times. In the event, the prince and his partner were handed out a thorough drubbing, with the players whose combined age was more than a hundred years turning out easy winners – 6-1, 6-3, 6-2. Many call it one of the most 'public defeats of all time', given the sizeable audience at Court 2. This remains royalty's only on-court appearance at Wimbledon.

Long Jump and High Jump… For Horses!

The equestrian events of the 1900 Olympics included two unusual events – a long jump and high jump for horses. Interestingly, the horses and their riders did not perform as well as humans – the long jump winner recorded a distance of 6.10 metres and the high jump winners cleared a height of 1.85 metres. The winner of the men's long jump leapt 7.18 metres while the winner of the high jump cleared 1.90 metres!

A Diving Long Jump

A very interesting event at the 1904 Olympics was something called plunge for distance. It was a swimming long jump of sorts. Contestants had to jump into the water from a standing position, and the distance they reached after 60 seconds or the point when they surfaced would be measured. William Dickey won with a distance of 19.61 metres.

Climb a Pole, Run across Boats, Swim under Boats… Win an Olympic Medal

The 1900 Olympics at Paris featured one of the most unusual swimming events. It was called the swimming obstacle race, and participants had to climb a pole, then run across a row of boats and finally swim under another row of boats. It took place on the River Seine and was immensely popular but was not held again. Frederick Lane of Australia, who had also won the 200 metres freestyle swimming event, won this rather odd, if entertaining, event.

The Boer War Exhibits Who Ran the Marathon

The 1904 Olympics were held at St. Louis in the US. The city was also hosting a massive fair at the same time, and one of the attractions was a Boer War exhibit that featured two African tribesmen, Len Tauyame and Jan Mashiani. The two, however, made history when they entered the Olympic marathon event, becoming the first Africans to participate in the Olympics. They both registered as representing their tribe (Tswana), and Tauyame finished ninth. He might have done better had he not been chased off course by a dog!

When Boxing Was Not Allowed in the Olympics

Boxing has been a part of the Olympic Games since its inclusion in 1904. The only time it was excluded was in 1912. The Olympics in that year were hosted in Stockholm, Sweden. And as boxing was banned by Swedish law, the event could not be held. It is believed that this led to the IOC limiting the power of the host nation to set the programme of the games!

The Longest Race in the Olympics

There are a number of long distance events in the Olympics – the 42-kilometre-long marathon, the 50 kilometres walk, and so on. But the longest race ever was at the 1912 Olympics at Stockholm. The men's individual team trial was a road race and spanned an astounding 320 kilometres or almost 199 miles. Rudolf Lewis of South Africa won the race in a time of 10 hours, 42 minutes and 39 seconds.

The Wrestling Bout That Went on for Almost Twelve Hours

Wrestling these days is fought over two rounds of three minutes each. However, in the early days of the sport, there were no time limits and bouts took place until one of the wrestlers pinned the other to the ground. This resulted in some VERY long wrestling bouts. Two of the longest of these took place in Greco-Roman wrestling in the 1912 Olympic Games at Stockholm. Anders Ahlgren of Sweden and Ivar Bohling of Finland grappled for nine hours in the final of the light-heavyweight category before the contest was declared a draw. In the middleweight category, the semi-final between Martin Klein of Estonia (then called Russia) and Finland's Alfred Asikainen lasted for 11 hours and 40 minutes before Klein finally won. However, the bout left Klein so drained that he was unable to compete in the final, and he had to concede the gold by a walkover.

The Most Populous Nation in the World, Only One Athlete at the Olympics

Liu Changchun took part in the 100 metres, 200 metres and 400 metres sprints at the 1932 Olympics at Los Angeles. He won no medals, and in fact, did not even qualify for the finals of any of the events. And yet he has a special place in Olympic history. He was the first athlete to represent the most populous nation in the world, China (Republic of China), at the Olympics. And the only one in that Olympics. China, with one of the largest populations in the world, had a solitary athlete in the 1932 Olympics.

Want to Be an Olympic Torchbearer? Run a Race

One of the greatest honours in sport today is carrying the Olympic torch into the stadium during the opening ceremony. However, for quite a while, the Olympic torchbearers were selected by a seemingly random process with the rationale that the torchbearer be a great athlete (Paavo Nurmi in 1952) or a symbol (Hiroshima-born Yoshiniro Sakai in 1964). The Italian Olympic committee decided to keep it simple for the 1960 Games at Rome – it organized a cross-country race. The winner would get to carry the Olympic torch. A young man called Giancalro Peris won and got to carry the flame. And has since been forgotten.

Just How Fast is the 'Fastest Person on Earth'?

The highest speed attained by a human being is 44.2 kmph (or 27.8 mph), recorded by Jamaica's Usain Bolt from the 60 metres to 80 metres mark of his world record 100 metres in the 2009 World Championships at Berlin. Bolt recorded a time of 9.58 seconds, which remains a world record at the time of writing, and his average speed over the distance was 37.58 kmph (or 23.35 mph). Does not sound too impressive in those terms, does it?

The Fastest Time Ever in the Marathon, but STILL not a World Record

At the time of writing, the fastest time ever recorded in a marathon is 1 hour, 59 minutes and 40 seconds, recorded by Eliud Kipchoge of Kenya in Vienna in 2019. It is the only time a human being has run the marathon in under two hours. However, this effort is not considered a world record because it was not recorded in a proper competition but at an event whose purpose was to break the two-hour mark in the marathon. Kipchoge was also assisted by a number of pacemakers to help him attain a greater speed, which is also not allowed. Kipchoge can therefore claim to be the only person to have run the marathon in under two hours but cannot quote his time as a world record.

Pollution is Bad for Cross-Country Running in the Olympics

Cross-country running was a part of the OIympic Games from 1912 to 1924. The event, however, was discontinued after 1924 when a majority of the runners were unable to finish the race. The 10,650 metres course was considered to be difficult with stony paths and weeds, but what made things really tough for the participants was the weather, with temperatures soaring to 40 degrees Celsius. To make matters worse, many runners were adversely affected by noxious fumes from a power plant near the course of the race. Only fifteen of the thirty-eight runners who started the race were able to finish, and most alarmingly, many actually went missing, resulting in medical teams from the Red Cross and the police searching for them. Many had passed out from the combination of the fumes and the heat. The event was scrapped and has not been seen since in the Olympics, notwithstanding appeals from a number of African nations that it be reinstated.

Why is a Dunk Shot Called a Dunk? Coffee!

The dunk is one of the most spectacular shots in basketball and involves a player catching the ball and literally slamming it through the basket with one or both hands instead of throwing it. Why is it called a dunk, though? Well, because in 1936, Pulitzer Prize winning writer Arthur Daley, on seeing it in 1936, wrote that the players had 'pitch[ed] the ball downward into the hoop, much like a cafeteria customer dunking a roll in coffee'. Chick Hearn, a Los Angeles Lakers announcer, is credited with adding a new dimension to the term by calling particularly emphatic dunk shots 'slam dunks'.

Women Boxed at the Olympics… In 1904!

Boxing became a full-fledged event for women in the 2012 Olympic Games. But rather remarkably, it had featured as a demonstration sport in 1904. This is remarkable when you consider that this was a period when women were considered too weak.

When Fencing in the Olympics Led to a Real Duel

Fencing at the 1924 Olympics resulted in an actual duel. Oreste Puliti of Italy, one of the favourites in the sabre event, was disqualified after an argument with the judges. An annoyed Puliti challenged one of the judges, Kovacs of Hungary, to a duel. They met at the Italy–Yugoslav border and fought for over an hour, injuring each other before the duel was finally stopped.

The Astounding Move That Is Banned in Gymnastics

In the 1972 Olympic Games, Olga Korbut of the USSR shocked people with an amazing move on the uneven bars. In it, Korbut stood on the higher bar, executed a backflip and then grabbed the bar again. Although spectacular, it was deemed too dangerous and was banned from gymnastics. It is called the Dead Loop.

Yes, Rope Climbing Was Part of Gymnastics at the Olympics

One of the eight events included in gymnastics in the 1896 Olympic Games was, rather interestingly, rope climbing. The other events, fortunately, were more routine. The home crowd was delighted with the rope climbing, though – the winner was a Greek, Nikolaos Andriakopoulos. The event was included in the 1904, 1924 and 1932 Olympics too and was then discontinued.

The Sport Especially Created for the Olympics

The Olympic Games mostly comprised sports that were popular and were already in existence. One sports event, however, can claim to have been totally created for the Olympics and began in the Games. This is the modern pentathlon, perhaps the most versatile sport in the world as it comprises fencing, swimming, horse riding, shooting and running. Credit for inventing the sport is given to Baron Pierre de Coubertin (the father of the modern Olympics), who is believed to have based it on the experience of a cavalry soldier behind enemy lines. The sport started in the Olympics, and the IOC even directly administered it until 1948.

Duelling Was a Proper Event at the Olympics

The early editions of the modern Olympic Games had some rather interesting – and shocking – events. One of these was duelling, which was seen at the Intercalated Games of 1906 and the 1908 Olympics. While the 1906 Games had contestants firing from duelling pistols at plaster dummies, the 1908 Games saw a more serious form of duelling with contestants firing at each other using duelling pistols loaded with wax bullets. Protective equipment was evidently worn for the 'torso, face and hands', and thankfully, there were no injuries. France won the gold, and the event was discontinued thereon.

Those Cans Tennis Balls Come in? They Are Special

The balls used in most sports are stored in generally conventional packaging (wraps, boxes and so on). However, tennis balls are kept in special pressurized cans (which is why you get a 'pop' sound when they open) to ensure they stay as good as new for as long as possible. Tennis balls are changed frequently during a match.

Who Is the Player in the NBA Logo?

The logo of the National Basketball Association (NBA) is one of the most famous in sport as it represents the sport's most famous and prestigious tournament. The logo is half blue and half red and has the silhouette of a player running with a ball in his hand. Not too many know that this silhouette is not a creation of an artist's imagery but is actually based on the photograph of a real player, Jerry West of Los Angeles Lakers, snapped by Wen Roberts.

The Table Tennis Rally That Just Went on and on

Table tennis has seen some long and thrilling rallies, but nothing ever comes close to the one that opened the match between Alex

Ehrlich of Poland and Paneth Farcas of Romania at the World Table Tennis Championships at Prague in 1936. The two players began their match by sending the ball back and forth for an astonishing 2 hours and 12 minutes. Ehrlich, who was known as one of the greatest defensive players of his time, actually switched the bat from his right hand to his left after 70 minutes. After 85 minutes of the rally, the umpire had to be replaced. Farcas finally lost the point, succumbing to fatigue in his arm as per some reports. The rally is believed to have lasted more than 12,000 strokes and many believe was the reason why time restrictions were brought into table tennis.

The Most Marked Playing Area in Sport

Most playing areas come with some marking or the other – football grounds have lines on the ground, cricket pitches have creases and so on – but no sport has as many markings on its playing area as American football, also called 'gridiron'. There are lines on every five yards of the 120-yard pitch and are also accompanied by large numbers every 10 yards!!

Ban the Sport First, Then Dominate It

The US is one of the most successful nations in the history of boxing. Many of the great champions in the sport have come from the US – Muhammad Ali, Mike Tyson, Joe Louis, Rocky Marciano and so on. The irony is that the US was very slow to adopt boxing. The sport was banned in the country till 1896 and was actually considered illegal. In 1896, it was legalized in New York, and the rest, as they love to say, is history.

A Match That Lasted… Four Seconds!

Not too many sporting events have finished as quickly as the Golden Gloves boxing contest between Michael Collins and Pat

Brownson in Minnesota in 1947. Barely had the crowd settled in than Collins knocked out Brownson with the very first punch of the bout and was declared the winner. At four seconds, it is one of the shortest sporting events ever.

Why Do Races Take Place in Anticlockwise Directions?

One of the curious facts of a lot of racing – from athletics to horse racing to motor cars and bikes – is that they take place in an anticlockwise direction. This was not always so. In fact, in the first few Olympic Games, races were run in a clockwise direction. However, in the years that followed, athletes switched to running anticlockwise. No clear reason has been given for this, with a number of theories existing. One is that as humans mostly read in an anticlockwise direction (from left to right), they would find it easier to view a race run in that format. Another is that as most people start running with the right foot, they are naturally oriented towards running anticlockwise. There are also theories about the rotation of the earth, but there's no official reason available for this anticlockwise movement.

Why Is Football Called 'Soccer'?

Football is known as 'soccer' in the US and some other countries. Some say that this is to distinguish it from 'gridiron football' or 'American football'. But why 'soccer'? Well, evidently the sport was called 'association football' early on. This became "assoc football" and in due course, 'Soccer'.

The Only Thing about Cricket That Has Not Changed

Cricket has seen a number of changes over the years. In fact, according to some experts, the only part of the sport that has not seen any changes or modifications is the length of the pitch it is played on – it has remained 22 yards.

Robin Hood Is Not Just a Hero but Also an Archery Skill

Almost everyone knows Robin Hood as the legendary archer of Sherwood Forest, who robbed the rich to feed the poor. However, Robin Hood is also an archery term and refers to the time when an arrow shot by an archer at the target splits an arrow already lodged there. According to legend, Robin Hood did just that at a fair!

The Athletics Events That Take Place in a Cage!

Most athletic events take place in large, open areas inside stadiums. Two events are, however, always held in semi-closed spaces. These are the discus throw and the hammer throw, where athletes have to participate from a semi-closed area called 'cage' with only one opening through which they can throw the discus or hammer. This is done to ensure that spectators and officials do not get hurt by the discus or hammer.

The Race That Starts from Outside the Oval Track

All races in athletics are run within an oval track that measures 400 metres outdoors and 200 metres indoors. However, one race actually starts from outside this oval track. This is the 110 metres hurdles, which is run in a straight line, but because of its rather unusual distance, has to start from outside the normal track, which measures 100 metres in a straight line!

Going Fencing? Wear White!

Cricket was considered to be the sport most associated with white uniforms but has now moved to more colourful apparel. One sport, however, that still largely sticks to white uniforms is fencing. This is because in the early days of the sport, the tips of the swords used by the participants were dipped in ink and the only way to find out if a person had been 'touched' was to see the mark of the tip on their uniform. Of course, technology for touch detection has become more sophisticated, but the white uniforms continue.

Fencing

The Oddest Racing Distance

The men's 110 metres hurdles is the only track event beyond 100 metres that does not have at least two zeroes in it. Why is the distance 110 metres and not something like 100 metres (like it is for the women)? There does not seem to be any clear reason. The race was initially run out 100 metres but then was increased to 120 metres by Oxford and Cambridge Universities. Evidently, the number was 'rounded off' to 110 metres by France in 1888, which is where it has stayed.

The Jump Is the Smallest Part of the Triple Jump!

The triple jump athletic event involves athletes going through three distinct movements – a hop, a step and finally a jump. There are many who refer to the event as 'Hop, Step and Jump' too. Many think that as the jump phase sees athletes flying through the air with both feet extended in front of them, the jump is actually the longest part of the triple jump. The truth is rather different. In fact, the hop is the longest part of the jump, accounting for about 37 per cent of the final distance, the step accounts for another 33 per cent, and finally the jump itself, while looking the most spectacular, generally makes up about 30 per cent of the final distance.

The Athletics Event That Requires the Least Space

Most athletics events require space for the athletes to run, throw and land. The one that requires the least space is actually the high jump, which generally has a run up area of about 12-15 metres and a landing area of a few metres of cushioned foam, with a thin bar and stand.

Why Are Basketballs Orange?

If you were wondering why the ball used in basketball is so often orange in colour, the reason is simple – good old visibility. The ball used to be dark brown for quite a while but was often difficult to spot, not just for the crowd but also for the players and the referees. According to some sources, Tony Hinkle, the head basketball coach of Butler University, experimented with a bright, orange ball in the 1950s, and the move was such a success that most matches these days use orange balls!

The Only Country with No National Football Team

They do not call football a universal sport for nothing. Each of the 193 nations registered in the United Nations has a national football team to represent it. There is one exception – the Marshall Islands in the Pacific Ocean. However, at the time of writing, football is believed to be finally catching on in this tiny country, which comprises a group of islands and has a population that is a little over 40,000!

Don't Drink and Drive... Or Shoot

Mention illegal substances and performance-enhancing drugs in sport, and most folks think of complex chemical substances manufactured in secrecy in laboratories and carefully fed to athletes to avoid detection. Well, those do exist. But those are not the only substances that are banned. Even having a drink before an archery event could cost you a medal – alcohol is banned in archery as it is seen to calm down nerves and help a contestant shoot straighter. Rather interestingly, the ban on alcohol is not as strict in rifle and pistol shooting events, although some competitions still have it in place.

Fastest Moving Object in Sport

What is the fastest moving object in the world of sport? It is evidently a badminton shuttlecock. A shuttlecock attained a staggering speed of 493 kmph during a racket testing session by Malaysia's Tan Boon Hoeng in 2017. The fastest a shuttle has gone in a match was from Pieler Kolding of Denmark, who smashed it at a speed of 426 kmph in the Badminton Premier League match in Bengaluru, India, in 2017. In contrast, a golf ball has attained a speed of about 330 kmph and a squash ball has gone at a speed of 281.6 kmph.

Fastest Ever in Formula One

Formula One racing is literally all about speed. But the fastest speed ever reached by a Formula One driver is 378 kmph by Valtteri Bottas, who hit that speed during qualifying for the European Grand Prix on the Baku City Circuit in 2016. Bottas also holds the record for the highest speed recorded during a Formula One race, hitting a speed of 372.5 kmph during the Mexico Grand Prix in 2016. The highest speed ever recorded by a Formula One car is 397.36 kmph recorded by the Honda team in 2006!

The Only Team to Have Played in Every Football World Cup

The football World Cup (also called the FIFA World Cup) was first played in 1930, and at the time of writing, had seen 22 editions. Remarkably, only one country has played in every edition of the World Cup. It is also the country most identified with football – Brazil. That apart, Germany has played in 20 tournaments and Argentina and Italy in 18 each.

Famous Football Teams and Their Nicknames

Most football teams have their own nicknames, which are given to them affectionately by the fans. Some of these are so popular that they are used to refer to the teams as often as the real names. Here are the nicknames of some of the most famous teams in the English Premier League:

Arsenal – Gunners
Everton – The Toffees
Manchester United – Red Devils
Liverpool – Reds

Aston Villa – The Villans
Brentford – The Bees
Brighton and Hove Albion – The Seagulls
Burnley – The Clarets
Chelsea – The Blues
Crystal Palace – The Eagles
Fulham – The Cottagers
Manchester City – The Citizens
Newcastle – The Geordies
Sheffield United – The Blades
West Ham – The Hammers
Luton – The Hatters

(Teams in leagues of other countries also have nicknames, but they are not in English)

Highest Earning Sportspersons!

Sport at the highest level can be an excellent paymaster, be it in terms of prize money or in terms of endorsements and other agreements. The richest sportspersons in the world often make a very pretty penny. As per *Forbes* magazine, these were the highest-paid athletes of the world in 2023:

Name	Sport	Total Earnings (USD Millions)	On-Field (USD Millions)	Off-Field (USD Millions)
1. C. Ronaldo	Football	136	46	90
2. L. Messi	Football	130	65	65
3. K. Mbappé	Football	120	100	20
4. LeBron James	Basketball	119.5	44.5	75
5. C. Alvarez	Boxing	110	100	10
6. D. Johnson	Golf	107	102	5
7. P. Mickelson	Golf	106	104	2
8. S. Curry	Basketball	100.4	48.4	52

9. R. Federer	Tennis	95.1	0.1	95
10. K. Durant	Basketball	89.1	44.1	45

Cristiano Ronaldo

Lionel Messi

Kylian Mbappé

Interestingly, tennis legend Roger Federer makes the list even though he announced his retirement and hardly played. As you can see, he made just 0.1 million USD from his on-field performance, but raked in a staggering USD 95 million from off-field ones.

Roger Federer

The Only Woman in the List of 50 Wealthiest Sportspersons!

If you wish to know about the difference in payments made to male and female athletes, you just need to cast a look at the *Forbes* 2023 list of World's Highest Paid Athletes. Of the fifty athletes mentioned in the list, only one is a woman – tennis legend Serena Williams, who stands 49th in the list with total earnings of USD 45.3 million, less than a third of what the highest-paid athlete in the world earns, despite being considered an all-time great.

The Most Valuable Sports Teams in the World

It is not just individuals. Sports teams command a fair bit of money too, and many are valued at billions of dollars and are major brands in their own right. As per the *Forbes* 2023 list, these are the ten most valuable sports teams in the world:

Team	**Sport**	**Value**
	(USD Billion)	
1. Dallas Cowboys	American Football	9
2. New York Yankees	Baseball	7.1
3. Golden State Warriors	Basketball	7
3. New England Patriots	American Football	7
5. Los Angeles Rams	American Football	6.9
6. New York Giants	American Football	6.8
7. Chicago Bears	American Football	6.3
8. Las Vegas Raiders	American Football	6.2
9. New York Knicks	Basketball	6.1
9. New York Jets	American Football	6.1

It is interesting to note that the list is exclusively made up of US teams, and that the ten wealthiest teams come from sports that are mainly popular in the US – gridiron (American) football, basketball and baseball. There are no cricket or association football (soccer) teams in the top ten, although Real Madrid is at 11th place and Manchester United at 13th.

First Sport on Film… And Edison Was behind the Camera

Sports is an integral part of many of our TV and video viewing schedules today. But a sport was first filmed way back in 1894, when Thomas Edison (yes, the same one credited with inventing the light bulb) filmed a boxing bout between Gentleman Jim Corbett and Peter Courtney at Edison's Black Maria Studio. The bout comprised six rounds of one minute each, and the footage of the first round is the oldest surviving sports footage in the world today.

Rowing Champs Who Sued Zuckerberg over Facebook

Twin brothers Cameron and Taylor Winklevoss were a superb rowing pair who were part of the Harvard men's eight that won the US national championships and were also part of the team that finished sixth in the World Cup in 2006. They also finished sixth in the coxless pair event at the Beijing Olympics in 2008. However, the Winklevoss twins are best known for their legal dispute with Mark Zuckerberg, whom they sued in 2004, claiming that he had stolen the idea of Facebook from their own software called ConnectU. They lost.

Played Badly? Off with the Hair!

Disappointment after a poor performance can take many shapes, but in at least two very famous cases, it lead to shaven heads. The Japansese wrestling team at the 1960 Olympics at Rome was so upset with its performance that all its members had their heads shaven. No less extreme was the reaction of Elvira Ozolina of the erstwhile USSR four years later at Tokyo. The world record holder and favourite in the women's javelin event committed four fouls to finish fifth. So upset was she that she went to the hairdresser in the Olympic Village and asked to have her head shaved. A shocked hairdresser refused to do so initially, but had to step in when Ozolina starting chopping off her long hair herself. She even refused to wear a scarf over her bald head.

Different Official Sports for Different Seasons

Canadians are known to love their sport. But what many do not know is that the country actually has two official sports. In winter, not surprisingly, the official sport of the massive nation is ice hockey. But when the snows melt and the sun shines in summer, the official sport of the nation changes to lacrosse!

The Fight that Inspired *Rocky*

When it comes to films with a sports theme, there are not too many that can match the popularity of the *Rocky* series, which revolves around the career of a fictional boxer called Rocky Balboa, with legendary Hollywood star, Sylvester Stallone in the lead role. However, not many know that the series was actually inspired by a real boxing contest between the legendary Muhammad Ali and a relatively unknown boxer called Chuck Wepner in 1975. Although no one gave Wepner a chance, he took Ali to the distance across fifteen rounds and even knocked him down for a short while. The bout is believed to have inspired Stallone to come out with the concept of Rocky, although the name of the boxer and his style of fighting is supposed to be a tribute to heavyweight boxing great, Rocky Marciano! Stallone initially denied that the Ali-Wepner fight had inspired *Rocky*, but admitted later that it had indeed done so.

A Legendary Career Saved by a Sharp-eyed Uncle

When it comes to cricket in general, and Indian cricket in particular, Sunil Gavaskar has a special place. He was the first player to score more than ten thousand runs in Test cricket and also the first player to ever score thirty Test centuries. However, none of that might have happened but for a sharp-sighted relative. After he was born (on 10 July 1949), his uncle Narayan Masurekar, noticed that he had a little hole near the top of his left earlobe. When Masurekar came to see him at the maternity home later, he was shocked to see that the baby who was supposed to be in Gavaskar's crib actually had no such feature in his left ear. A hunt was launched and Gavaskar was eventually discovered sleeping next to a fisherwoman. The staff at the maternity home had got the babies mixed up after bathing them. On such gifts of vision does the cricket history depend!

Image Copyright Information

Index

SCORE <5072> HIGH SCORE <20463>

GAME OVER

<CONTINUE>

Quick facts for comprehensive knowledge!

Chambers has been a staple name in lexicographic and general reference since 1872, known for their dictionary range, encyclopaedic works, companions and fact books.

Hachette India has launched the Chambers Facts books, in India – a quick reference series meant for professionals, students, job test candidates, quizzers, trivia afficionados and any curious minds. Election, Cinema, Cricket, Football, Sports, World History and many more from the series.